THE MIRACLES OF
ARCHANGEL
MICHAEL

ALSO BY DOREEN VIRTUE

THE MIRACLES OF
ARCHANGEL
MICHAEL

Doreen Virtue

HAY HOUSE, INC.
Carlsbad, California • New York City
London • Sydney • Johannesburg
Vancouver • Hong Kong • New Delhi

Published and distributed in the United States by: Hay House, Inc.: www.
hayhouse.com • **Published and distributed in Australia by:** Hay House Australia
Pty. Ltd.: www.hayhouse.com.au • **Published and distributed in the United
Kingdom by:** Hay House UK, Ltd.: www.hayhouse.co.uk • **Published and
distributed in the Republic of South Africa by:** Hay House SA (Pty), Ltd.: www.
hayhouse.co.za • **Distributed in Canada by:** Raincoast: www.raincoast.com •
Published in India by: Hay House Publishers India: www.hayhouse.co.in

Editorial supervision: Jill Kramer   *Design:* Jen Kennedy

Library of Congress Cataloging-in-Publication Data

Virtue, Doreen.
  The miracles of Archangel Michael / Doreen Virtue. -- 1st ed.
    p. cm.
  ISBN 978-1-4019-2205-4 (hardcover) -- ISBN 978-1-4019-2206-1 (tradepaper)
  1. Michael (Archangel) 2. Angels--Miscellanea. I. Title.
  BF1623.A53V573 2008
  202'.15--dc22
                                          2008012623

ISBN: 978-1-4019-2206-1

12 11 10 09   7 6 5 4
1st edition, November 2008
4th edition, September 2009

Printed in the United States of America

To Archangel Michael,
with eternal gratitude.

CONTENTS

INTRODUCTION

This is a nondenominational book about the archangel named Michael, a powerful celestial being who protects, guides, repairs, and heals. Michael interacts with and affects the physical world from his nonphysical dimension. At times, as you'll read about in this book, he even appears as a three-dimensional person.

Archangel Michael is God's right-hand man in enacting the purpose of bringing peace to Earth by eradicating fear and stress. Michael's ingenious methods are unlimited, as is his ability to be with multiple people simultaneously. Since he is unlimited, Michael is available—indeed, he prefers—to help you and everyone with any situation that engenders peace.

The term *archangel* (pronounced: *ARK-an-gel*) is derived from the Greek phrase "the greatest messenger of God." *Arch* means "the first" or "the greatest," and *angel* means "messenger of God." Michael's name is Hebrew and Babylonian for "he who is like God." So *Archangel Michael* means "the greatest messenger, who is like God."

In other words, Michael brings pure messages of love, wisdom, and power directly from the Creator.

Michael is the only angel accorded the "archangel" title in the Bible, where he's also called "one of the chief princes." The books of Daniel and Revelations describe how Michael provides protection during times of trouble.

Countless legends, particularly in Christian, Judaic, Islamic, and Celtic traditions, discuss Archangel Michael's renowned strength and wisdom. Yet, this archangel isn't merely relegated to the pages of sacred texts. He's very much alive and among us today. In fact, chances are good that he has helped *you*, especially if you've called upon him. He may have even guided you to this book.

Before we go further, though, I want to clarify a couple of points:

1. **Michael doesn't want to be worshipped.** He gives all the glory to God and doesn't want to be prayed to. He's an intercessor between the Creator and created (that is, *us*). So we call upon him without praying to him, which is a subtle but important distinction.

2. **Michael is unlimited.** He's able to simultaneously be with everyone having unique and individual experiences. So never worry that you're bothering him with a so-called small request. Michael aspires to help humans achieve world peace, one person at a time. So he wants to give you assistance with whatever brings *you* peace.

Although Michael is associated with certain religions, the truth is that he helps everyone. He loves all people unconditionally, just as God does. Yet as powerful as he is, Michael is only allowed to intervene in your life if you give him permission, since he can't violate your free will. So he does need you to ask for help before he can offer it.

Writing this book immersed me in the habit of calling upon Archangel Michael. I admire the writers of the stories contained herein, as they all had the presence of mind to call upon Michael during times of trouble. It's so easy when something happens to say "Darn!" (or something even harsher). It's a much more productive habit to simply exclaim: "Archangel Michael!"

God and the angels, including Michael, respond to any call for help. So you can ask aloud, silently, in writing, or in song. You can request his assistance through a traditional invocation, an affirmation, or even a "Help, Michael!" The important point isn't *how* you ask, but that you do so.

So why call upon Michael when you can petition God directly for help? It's certainly best to follow your religious and spiritual beliefs, and if you feel it's preferable to talk only with God, then that's definitely your best path. What I've learned is that when we ask for the Creator's assistance, angels are the messengers who intervene. So in other words, the results are the same whether we solicit Michael or God for the help. You can ask the Almighty to send Michael to you, or you can call upon the archangel directly.

Since Michael's primary role is protection (he's the patron saint of police officers and military personnel), he guards you from lower energies. If you ever worry about the integrity of people or spirits, call upon him. Like a sacred nightclub bouncer, Michael ensures that only beings of pure love and light come near you. Assisted by a legion of angels known as the "Band of Mercy," Michael also works with Jesus, saints, and other archangels and religious deities.

Most of those who've contributed their stories to this book have seen, felt, or heard Archangel Michael. You'll notice that they didn't *do* anything to invoke this visitation except ask for his help without attachment to *how* it would occur. When you ask for Archangel Michael's aid, he always says yes . . . and you can count on his assistance occurring in a perfect *and* surprisingly delightful way.

In the next four chapters, we'll explore how this celestial being connects with us through our physical senses. *Your* Archangel Michael encounter will very likely be similar to the stories in this book, yet with its own unique variations. That's because Michael follows the most complex, precise, and amazing computer in the universe: the Divine and infinite wisdom of God. So, every Michael interaction and rescue is tailor-made for the particular person and circumstance.

CHAPTER ONE

SEEING MICHAEL

Countless paintings of Archangel Michael depict him as a muscular winged deity with Nordic-looking features, standing atop a mountain peak and holding a sword and shield.

The descriptions of those who have glimpsed the archangel match these paintings very closely. When people see Michael, they usually describe him as very tall, with radiant or exotic eyes. He isn't exactly blond and tan, as paintings generally portray, since he doesn't have hair or skin—but the golden light that emanates from him makes him appear summery in coloring.

While Michael will always appear when you call, you're more likely to feel his presence than observe him with your eyes. But if you do see him, the stories in this chapter can give you insights into his visual appearance.

Children See Angels

Babies and young people are highly aware of the presence of angels. Watch infants and you'll see them scan the outline of their parents, focusing on the pretty dancing lights around their mothers' shoulders (which are guardian angels!). While babies seem to smile for no reason, I believe that their happiness comes from seeing the angels who have accompanied them on their journey from Heaven.

So-called imaginary friends are really angels that children can see and hear. When parents listen to their kids' angel stories with respect and open-mindedness, the adults help their offspring trust their intuition. Because children's minds and hearts are open to new experiences, they easily connect with angels. In fact, a 1980s Ohio State University study found that children had the highest number of verifiable psychic experiences, compared to other age-groups.

I believe that children are great spiritual teachers! Just as young Joan of Arc and Bernadette of Lourdes contributed greatly to the world by listening to the Divine voice despite strong criticism, so can we learn a great deal from children's insights.

I find it especially fascinating that these youngsters, such as Sandra Slaght's daughter Meryn, describe classic Michael features without having seen paintings or heard descriptions of him! Sandra explains:

> I was in the middle of a divorce and a friend had recently given me a copy of Doreen's book *Healing with the Angels*. We'd just moved out of

our family home and into a new rental. My three-year-old daughter, Meryn, was frightened to sleep in her new room, so she climbed into bed with me. I'd just finished reading about Archangel Michael in the book, and I explained to Meryn that anytime she felt afraid, she could call upon him to protect her.

She then exclaimed, "Oh yeah!" as if to ask why *she* didn't think of that first, and then proceeded to say, "Yeah, Mommy, he's the one with the big sword."

Before reading about him in Doreen's book, I didn't even know he carried a big sword! So there was no way for Meryn to know about Michael's signature blade unless she saw him herself!

Children's accounts of the archangel offer us reassurance that we adults aren't just seeing visions of Michael and his sword as a result of preconceived expectations.

Parents frequently ask me how to help their children who have night terrors or insomnia due to frightening images in their bedrooms. These little ones aren't just imagining monsters in their closets or alligators under their beds. Children's sensitivity sometimes attracts earthbound spirits who wander among the living after death. While these entities usually don't cause harm, their presence can upset sensitive people.

I believe it's essential for parents to teach their children about Archangel Michael, who can keep earthbound spirits away. Kids are empowered when they know that they can ask him for physical and spiritual protection, as three-year-old Celeste Amour learned from her mother, who tells the following story:

My three-year-old daughter, Celeste, tells my husband and me about various people who have come to her and the special friends she meets that we know to be spirits. I've always encouraged her to call upon her angels for help and have had many open conversations about how these beings protect us all.

Recently, Celeste was going through a troubled time with a spirit man she kept seeing. This resulted in night traumas and her refusing to go to sleep. She complained that "the man with a hole in his neck" kept coming to her.

Being only three, Celeste was obviously frightened and couldn't make sense of the visitor. I encouraged her to call her angels and said protective prayers, which temporarily worked. However, it wasn't long before the man was back and Celeste was so distressed!

So I called a spiritual practitioner for support. He advised me on how to call upon Archangel Michael and said that the man Celeste was seeing hadn't passed over particularly well and was seeking her out for help.

That night, my daughter became terrified, not wanting to go to sleep, as the spirit man would come. I explained that if he arrived, she must ask Archangel Michael to help her and to tell the visitor to go to the light.

In the morning, Celeste hugged me and immediately announced, "The man with the hole is gone." She then said, "Angel Michael flew into my room! He lay down with me. I rested inside his wing, and he said, 'Don't cry, Celeste,' and I slept."

This was the most beautiful thing I'd ever heard, and I was overwhelmed with joy for her. Archangel Michael quickly became Celeste's new buddy, and the man with the hole hasn't been seen since.

Although it's both healthy and helpful for parents to teach their children about angels (particularly how to call upon the archangel Michael during stressful situations), it's sometimes not necessary. Very often, children learn about Michael because he and the other heavenly helpers visit and teach them directly, as happened with Maria Taylor's daughter:

When my daughter, Rachael, was seven years old, we were looking at a picture of an angel. She asked me who he was. I said, "I'm not sure, but I think it could be Archangel Uriel."

"Well, it's not Archangel Michael—I know that!" Rachael said with conviction.

"Oh, it isn't?" I asked. "How do you know that, then, Rachael?"

She looked at me as though I should know better and said matter-of-factly, "Because it doesn't look like him!"

My curiosity piqued, I replied, "Okay, honey,

how do you know what he looks like?" I was trying hard not to sound as if I was a disbeliever and was choosing my words carefully so that I wasn't influencing my daughter at all.

But I needn't have worried, as Rachael simply said, "Because I've seen him."

"So, honey, when did you see him?" I asked.

She explained, "When I was frightened one night and trying to be brave. I was really scared, and I saw a man who had a glowing white light around him."

"Did that frighten you, Rachael?" I asked.

"No," she responded, "because he said not to be afraid."

I leaned in and asked, "But how do you know that it was Michael?"

She looked me squarely in the eyes and replied, "Because he told me who he was when I asked him! He tucked me into bed and said, 'Do not be afraid. I am Michael.'"

Rachael sleeps peacefully, with the reassurance that Archangel Michael is watching over her.

You can talk openly with your children about how to call upon Archangel Michael for protection. You and your child can work with him in conjunction with your religious traditions—for instance, asking God to send Michael or requesting the presence of both Jesus and Michael. The archangel is nondenominational, so he's happy to help any- and everyone.

Here are some suggested age-appropriate ways to start a discussion about angels with your child:

- **Preschool:** Read a children's book about angels together. Point to the pictures, ask your son or daughter questions, and allow him or her to speak freely. Answer your child's questions honestly.

- **Grade school:** Draw pictures together of people and angels while having a discussion about how you and your child feel about these heavenly messengers and whether you've had any experiences with them. (Keep your side of the conversation very uplifting, and avoid talking about anything that could frighten the child.)

- **Junior high school:** Watch a movie or television show with an angel theme, and discuss your honest reactions to it with each other. Allow your child to express opinions freely.

- **High school:** Listen to a modern song about angels together, such as "Calling All Angels" by Train, "Angel" by Sarah McLachlan, or "She Talks to Angels" by the Black Crowes.

During your discussion, the important points are:

1. You, the parent, are willing to listen to your child's feelings and thoughts about angels with an open mind. Once children feel that you've heard them, they're much more open to listening to your teachings and advice.

2. Tell your child about Archangel Michael and how he's available to help anyone who asks.

3. There are many equally effective ways to call upon Michael. Your child can say or think the archangel's name, look at a painting of him, wish for him to come, color a drawing of him, or write his name on a piece of paper to put under the pillow. Michael is the most powerful angel, and he's completely unlimited, so trust that he will respond to your child's call. He'll ensure that only angels of God's pure love are with your little one.

4. Once your son or daughter calls upon Michael, fear generally subsides rapidly, as his very presence has a calming effect.

5. Ask your child to talk to you about experiences with Michael and to come to you with any questions.

Seeing Signs from Michael

More than seeing the actual angel, most people see evidence of Michael's presence. He's a very clear communicator, and you're likely to hear his guidance in your mind or sense it as a gut feeling. However, just to get his point across, Michael also sends physical signs such as feathers so that you'll trust that your guidance is real.

You can say to Michael: "Please send me a sign in the physical world that I will easily notice and understand," or words to that effect. Don't specify what type of sign you want; leave that decision to the angels. Once you ask for one, it *will* appear—it's just a matter of noticing it. As Susan discovered, though, most signs from Michael are crystal clear:

> My son, Sean, and I went to our local park together the night before he was to leave on a 15-day trip to Australia with other People to People Student Ambassadors who had just finished fifth, sixth, or seventh grade. At first, I worried that Sean was too young to participate in such a journey so far away from home.
>
> But my worry was tempered by Sean's obvious enthusiasm for the wonders he was to experience in touring Australia, and with this knowledge, a strong inner peacefulness enveloped me. I knew that I was meant to let things take their course and to stop worrying. Sure enough, every obstacle was overcome as we planned and paid for his trip.
>
> So there I was in the park, savoring the last moments with my son, engraving a mental picture

of him playing in the creek, when—wiping away a tear—I asked God for a clear sign that Sean would return home safely.

I received that answer rather quickly when we turned around to walk to the car. There, lying in the middle of the street just behind me, was a holy card with a picture of Michael the archangel on it. We hadn't seen it on our way to the creek moments before, and no one was around us during that time. After that, we both knew we had no worries. And we didn't!

A lot of times, Michael sends signs just to help us know that he's with us and to reduce fears of being alone or unguided. Stories such as the following from Liv Lane make me think of Archangel Michael as an artist who signs his work:

> For several weeks, my young son had been having trouble sleeping because he sensed unkind beings in his bedroom. We tried all sorts of things to ease his fears, but he still couldn't sleep. I felt desperate to find him help (and get us *all* some sleep!) but didn't know where to turn next.
>
> Then one afternoon while I was running errands, I thought of Archangel Michael and started asking him for guidance and assistance with my son. I pulled over into a parking lot to collect my thoughts and suddenly noticed a small but bright rainbow in the sky. And then I started laughing, realizing that the rainbow was directly above a Michaels crafts store! I took it as a clever

sign from the archangel that he got my message and was happy to help.

Signs can also appear in response to questions that you pose. Whenever you feel stressed or conflicted, take a moment to ask God and the angels for guidance. They'll immediately answer you and often punctuate their message with a physical sign, as a woman named Oceanna discovered:

Archangel Michael is absolutely my favorite angel to connect with because he is such a strong, loving presence and because he has such an incredible sense of humor.

One of my favorite examples of this was when I was feeling very overwhelmed and vulnerable. I was in my car driving, talking to God and the angels about my feelings and really pouring my heart out.

"Oh, angels!" I sighed, a tear running down my cheek. "What am I supposed to do?"

Just as I uttered these words, something to my left caught my eye. It was a huge electronic billboard, and in great big flashing capital letters it said: ASK MICHAEL! In my upset condition, I'd forgotten to ask for his help!

I started to laugh, and my heart swelled with love for this great and beautiful being of light. I knew Archangel Michael was with me, and I received a wonderful healing of my broken heart. I felt so safe and loved in that moment, and right then and there I said a prayer of gratitude and asked for his intervention in my situation.

Within a day or two, everything was resolved. I found the courage to speak my truth and move on with my life. I know Michael stood beside me the entire time, wrapping me in his glorious wings. My relationship with the archangel continues to grow as I learn more from him every day. I never forget to ask for his help and guidance . . . but I know that if one day I do, he'll be right there to remind me!

The signs from the angels show their wonderful and loving sense of humor. Oceanna's was a literal sign, reminding her that God and the angels couldn't intervene and undermine her free will unless she first asked for help. I love this story because it's such a clear message from above.

But angelic signs aren't always as literal as Oceanna's. Sometimes they're more subtle, as was the case for Susie Sparks when she asked Michael for one:

The other day, I was getting ready to ride my bike. I'd made a commitment to exercise every morning, thinking that this would improve my attitude toward my nursing job. On this occasion in particular I was just plain down in the dumps.

So I was riding in the drizzling rain, whining in my mind about my job and wondering if the angels had heard my prayers. I said aloud, "Archangel Michael, please show me a sign that you're with me."

I turned the corner and there was a huge, bright, beautiful rainbow! I bowed my head with humility and stopped my bike to thank Archangel Michael. It may not seem that significant to some, but to me it was just what I needed.

As Susie said, the rainbow may not have been a clear enough sign for some people, but *she* knew what it meant. That's why it's important to notice and honor your internal reactions, as these inner clues can validate your angel messages.

Yet, many of the signs that Michael sends are cosmic and natural . . . such as a rainbow; angel-shaped clouds; and even a shooting star, as Laura Cohen experienced:

My son Jeremy and I were walking on a track at the local high school during a very dark summer night. Jeremy, who is 13 years old, said, "Mom, I'm scared. I feel some bad vibes."

I secretly agreed with him but didn't want to scare him. To ease his fears, I said, "Why don't we call upon Archangel Michael to protect us from all harm and guide us?" We summoned the great archangel together.

Jeremy, who was riding his bike around the track, pedaled ahead and left me walking behind him. As soon as he sped up in front of me, I saw the biggest, most spectacular shooting star make a complete arc over my son's head up in the dark heavens. There was no moonlight that night, so the streak of firelight was brilliantly amazing.

I instantly knew that Archangel Michael was answering our prayers. We were protected, and from that moment on, I kept walking around the track with a sense of complete peace and the knowledge that I was surrounded by the most wonderful warrior angel leading the way. Many times before when I've spoken to this great angel, a shooting star has been a heavenly affirmation that my prayers have been heard.

Since Archangel Michael is a protector, his signs are designed to comfort and reassure. He wants you to know that he's with you and that he hears your prayers and questions. If you don't trust or notice the signs that he sends, he'll communicate his message in different ways until you're at peace. You can also tell Michael that you don't see, understand, or trust what he's sending. The archangel appreciates your candor with him, and he's happy to help you recognize the signs.

Sometimes, to really drive home his message, Michael transmits multiple signs. He often includes his name like an artist's signature on many of his physical messages, as he did for a woman named Sarah on a long drive:

My brother, mother, and I were moving from Texas to California in a Jeep pulling a rented trailer. We'd never driven with one before and didn't realize what we were getting ourselves into until after we were on the road. I started out driving, but the trailer felt too unsteady as it swayed back and forth. Fearing that I'd lose control of the Jeep, my brother took over driving.

He seemed to get the hang of it and had a comfort level that I didn't have with the trailer. While he drove, I was in the backseat reading my angel books. I called upon Archangel Michael to protect us on our journey. Little did I know how much we would need it!

About an hour outside of Phoenix, we were driving at the highway's 80-mile-per-hour speed limit, when the trailer started fishtailing and my brother lost control of the car. We ended up in a ditch on the freeway's median strip. Somehow, the car was undamaged!

As we reentered the freeway, I looked up and saw "444" on a billboard, which I know means: "The angels are with you." Then, a semi truck drove by us with "444" on the license plate and the words *Michael Most* painted on its side. At that moment, I knew that Archangel Michael was guiding and protecting us. I saw that same "Michael Most" truck twice more on our journey, one of those times right before we reached our final destination.

After we got home, my brother did some research on trailers. He said that he didn't know how we made it home alive, since we'd violated many safety regulations by having a trailer attached. That validated all of my thoughts about our being guided home by Archangel Michael.

People frequently tell me that they pull Archangel Michael oracle cards from my 44-card decks as a sign that he's helping them. Since oracle cards are a physical way to communicate with the angels, it makes sense that Michael would reach out to us through the ones that carry his image and name. Elisabeth Roosendaal explained how she received her Archangel Michael oracle card before she understood its meaning and impact:

Archangel Michael has been making his presence known to me for some time now. Recently I did a card reading for myself using Doreen's *Archangel Oracle Cards* and pulled the Archangel Michael, "You Are Safe" card with the message: *I am protecting you against lower energies, and guarding you, your loved ones, and home.*

At the time, I couldn't see its relevance to the question I'd asked, but I appreciated the message just the same. The following evening, my brother and I went into the city with a friend and returned home several hours later to find the front door suspiciously wide open and the house in darkness. The two guys went inside to investigate, and my first thought was the card reading. I knew without a doubt that we were all safe and that everything within the house would be exactly as we had left it. And it was.

As with the authors of these stories, you can receive signs from God, Michael, and the other angels simply by asking a question or requesting a sign. The signs may come to you in a physical way, or you may even see Archangel Michael's glowing aura, as I'll discuss next.

Michael's Blue and Purple Lights

Everybody glows, whether they're a human, animal, or angel. This light radiates from our Creator's love and our souls' life force.

Guardian angels emit a beautiful pure-white radiance that some people see with their physical eyes. These "angel lights" look like sparkling shimmers or flashes of brightness (similar to a camera's flashbulb). They appear as white orbs on digital photographs (especially those taken at night) and on Kirlian (aura) cameras.

The archangels, who are larger and more powerful than guardian angels, have colored lights that correspond to each one's specific purpose. Archangel Michael's aura color is a royal purple that's so bright, it looks like cobalt blue. He also radiates a golden light that makes him appear tanned and blond.

This light is connected to Christ. Those who've seen Jesus in their prayers, meditations, dreams, and near-death experiences always talk about the golden illumination around his head. Look at any traditional painting of Jesus—you'll notice that artists see or sense this golden glow, too, as it's always around his head like a halo.

Since Michael is very connected to Christ (although he's not affiliated with any particular religion), the archangel has a golden glow very near to his form. Then there's a second layer of light around the first. This additional layer extends wide and far, and those who connect with Michael often report seeing sparkles or flashes of bright blue or purple.

Those who see "angel lights" are relieved to discover that their vision is accurate (many have told me that they got their eyes checked by ophthalmologists, who couldn't find any organic cause for this phenomenon).

The blue or purple sparkling lights are a sign that Michael is near, as a woman named Pushtie discovered:

> I'm an actress in India. One day as I was leaving for an early-morning film shoot, I asked Archangel Michael to watch over me and protect my home. I do this every morning, in addition to asking Michael the question: "Is there anything I need to do before I leave the house?"
>
> Many times in response to this question, I receive an intuitive feeling or thought to bring something that I've forgotten. But that day, I clearly heard Michael say that I hadn't switched off my bathroom water heater. I didn't believe him, because I'm always very careful to turn it off after my shower. So I began walking out of the house to go to work . . . but a purple light glowed in the doorway, practically blocking my way! I also noticed a warm temperature in that area.
>
> A chill ran down my spine as I had a mental image of my water heater bursting and the house catching on fire. So I decided to check the bathroom and was dumbfounded to discover that I *had* left the heater on! As I switched it off, my hand accidentally brushed the burning-hot body of the appliance. I realized that the heater would probably have burst within the hour.
>
> Thus, Archangel Michael helped me save my house.

I've also found that people who work with Michael are highly drawn to bright blue and vivid purple. So if you find yourself shopping for cobalt-blue drinking glasses or burying your face in a royal purple blanket, your attraction to these colors is a sign that you're working with the archangel.

Many people report seeing Michael's blue lights during a crisis, like the trails that Superman leaves behind when he swoops on the scene to save the day. This certainly was the case for Shirley Mischael-Morales, who was protected by Archangel Michael:

My two small children and I were traveling across a busy eight-lane freeway bridge when an accident brought traffic to a sudden halt in two of the lanes. Late for an appointment and frustrated that the vehicles to my left were traveling too quickly for me to change into that lane, I brought my car to a stop and glanced into the rearview mirror in time to observe a large vehicle approaching at a high speed.

The driver suddenly slammed on the brakes and the vehicle lost control, hit the guardrail, spun in a circle, and barreled toward my car. In a split second, a flash of blue light caught my attention and I saw Archangel Michael in the sky. The light was like a star bursting in my forehead.

Instantaneously, I was guided to take action. As my conscious awareness sped up, the physical world seemed to move in slow motion. With no time to check for oncoming traffic, I slammed

my foot onto the accelerator and sped into the lane to my left—barely in time to create just enough space for the out-of-control vehicle to pass through, sideswiping my car and hitting two others but successfully avoiding what could have been a deadly collision. Although life-threatening danger was present, Archangel Michael's guidance kept me calm. It very simply imparted clarity and precision of action.

The woman who was driving the vehicle that had lost control came running toward me. When she saw that there were children in my car, she embraced me and exclaimed, "Thank God they're alive! Thank God we're *all* alive!"

A man then approached and anxiously explained that he'd been traveling at a high speed in the lane I'd moved into until something had told him to change lanes quickly to make room for my car to get out of the other vehicle's path. Yet there was no logical reason for him to assume that in a split second a car that was completely stopped would suddenly bolt into his lane. He felt miraculously guided. There hadn't been enough time for the accident to be avoided except through heavenly intervention.

The experience was a powerful gift that affirmed the protective presence of Archangel Michael and my ability to receive his guidance and keep my children safe.

Not only did Shirley see Archangel Michael and his light, but she also received his direction as silent thoughts that guided her driving. The calmness that she felt in such an intensely dangerous situation is ample evidence of Divine intervention.

In the same way, Ursula Lovelock saw the blue-light evidence of Michael's lifesaving intervention. When you read her story, you can almost imagine the archangel swooping in and out so fast that only his light trail was visible:

> I've been using Archangel Michael's protection for myself and my family since discovering the angels back in 2002. Early in 2003, my son Tristan and I had just returned from a shopping trip. I parked the car in our garage and helped Tristan, who was two and a half at the time, out of his car seat.
>
> As we were walking out, I reached up and grabbed the heavy garage door and pulled it down, allowing its weight and momentum to swing it shut. I thought Tristan was standing behind me, but as the metal door picked up speed and began to fall, I suddenly felt an intuitive urge to grab it.
>
> Looking around for Tristan, I saw him standing directly beneath the door, with the hard metal only centimeters from his beautiful blond curls. In between it and his head, I saw Archangel Michael's calling card: four or five brilliantly vibrant blue sparkles dancing and lingering for a few moments before disappearing. I know that the door would have cracked Tristan's skull if it had fallen on him. Thank you, Archangel Michael!

As Ursula mentioned, she'd been asking for the archangel's help for several years, and she realized that he can't violate our free will by intervening without our permission. But once we ask for his help, step back—because Michael is coming through to save the day!

Tracy Hanratty's experience of having her car broken into is a perfect example. Michael couldn't protect her belongings because she hadn't asked for his help. But once Tracy called upon him for safety and protection, he immediately came to her, as evidenced by his telltale blue lights:

> One evening after work, I parked beside my house and then rushed inside because my son hadn't been feeling well. In my haste, I left some stuff in the car. When I went back outside to retrieve these things, I noticed that three of my windows had been smashed and the items had been stolen. I was totally shocked and couldn't believe this had happened.
>
> I felt vulnerable in my own home that evening, worried that the person who'd smashed the windows might still be nearby. I knew I wouldn't sleep much that night.
>
> But then I remembered Doreen advising people to ask Archangel Michael to position an angel to the north, south, east, and west of the house for protection. I did this, and that night I kept waking up and seeing flashes and lines of a very bright royal blue in my room. I wasn't afraid . . . but I *was* very much aware that I was protected, and I felt a sense of peace. I now ask

every night for angel protection for my home as well as for my car.

So Tracy learned from this experience, and now asks for angels to watch over her and her belongings, which is a healthy and smart habit to develop!

The only exception to the "free will" clause that angels must follow is if people are about to be killed before it's their time to go. God and the angels can intervene without someone's permission to save a life. Sometimes they do so directly, and other times they give the person Divine guidance to follow, as was the case for me when my life was threatened during an armed carjacking in 1995. If I hadn't followed that guidance, I might not be alive today.

But the question as to why some lives are miraculously saved and others aren't still remains an earthly mystery that we may not understand until we ascend beyond three dimensions. In any case, enough people do experience miraculous interventions to let us know that we're watched over and protected.

In the following story, Sheila didn't specifically ask for Archangel Michael's help, but because her life was endangered, he came to her rescue. Sheila credits him with saving her life, and she knows that *he* was her protector because of his signature blue light:

I was in a severe car accident when I was rear-ended by a truck while I was stopped at a traffic light. The truck's driver swerved at the last second and hit my car's right rear at about 80 miles per hour. My car lurched forward into oncoming traffic, where I was then sideswiped on the passenger side by another vehicle, which made mine spin in a circle.

I then saw a bright blue flash of light! My car was totaled, and the only area that wasn't smashed was the driver's side. I was taken to the hospital with cuts, bruises, and a broken collarbone.

I've since learned that the blue flash of light that I saw during the incident was the sign of Archangel Michael's presence. He sure did protect me that day, because the police, fire department, and doctors were amazed that I had as few injuries as I did and wasn't killed. Thank you, Michael!

If we're highly stressed, we become so internally focused that we block out the awareness of our angels' presence and messages. So people who need their heavenly helpers the most often can't hear them! Fortunately, the angels are highly creative and persistent in answering our prayers. Sometimes that means they work through a friend or family member, as happened to Penny Taylor:

I was having a down day. It was a rainy Sunday and I was depressed, so I decided to hibernate, watching television beneath my electric blanket. I experienced such a huge sense of darkness, energy depletion, and loss brought on by an ongoing battle with depression and personal grief. I felt lost and disconnected from God.

I sensed no other option but prayer, and as the tears rolled down my face, I asked with all my heart for some relief from my feelings. I prayed hard that Archangel Michael would give me a sign that he was indeed with me and hadn't abandoned me.

What happened next was pretty significant to me . . . and was also an instant answer to my prayer! A dear friend who lived some distance away from me text-messaged my cell phone and said: "I have no idea why, but I had a vision of you just now all completely dressed and surrounded in the most beautiful purple light. What does this mean? Are you okay?"

As I read the simple text, I was amazed and in awe. This friend wasn't one for saying such things, and she sent the message the instant after I'd asked for a sign from Archangel Michael.

Needless to say, my mood lifted, and I realized that it would have been a whole lot easier to have prayed and asked for help well before my mood had slipped into its dark shadows! We all deserve support and love from God and the angels. Just ask!

Penny's message to "just ask" is a great reminder, born of her successful experience with requesting a sign from Michael. The archangel always appears to us in exactly the right way for the situation and people involved . . . and sometimes this means that we clearly see him.

Seeing Michael in Dreams and Meditations

Many "Michael sightings" occur during dream time. We're more apt to see and hear an angel while we're sleeping because the fearful ego-mind is also asleep. Our hearts and minds are more open and less distracted while we're in this state, and we let go of "three-dimensional" thinking.

Sometimes people can't remember their nightly visions the next day because when they wake up, their dreamworld information doesn't make sense. Nonetheless, everything we learn during dreams is still in our unconscious mind, helping us along.

Some people see a representative of Michael, as in Eshantie's dream:

> I was feeling very alone as I struggled through a child-custody battle. One night before going to sleep, I talked with Archangel Michael and asked him to make his presence known to me, as I really needed some sort of confirmation that I wasn't alone in the universe.
>
> That night I dreamed of a childhood friend who'd died ten years earlier. His name was Michael. In the dream, I sat next to him and felt an all-encompassing calmness, and a feeling that everything was all right came over me.
>
> I believe that Archangel Michael used my dear old friend as a point of contact, as I had never dreamed about him before and haven't since.

Archangel Michael spoke to Eshantie in a way that her mind could accept. He's powerful yet always gentle, so if seeing an angel would frighten a person, he'll send a sign or a symbol.

We're more open to Michael and the other beings from Heaven when we're sleeping, yet we may not remember the angel visitations that occur at this time. We're more apt to recall these experiences when they occur in that in-between stage of waking and dreaming, as Emma Lee Quick discovered:

It was very early in the morning. I'd already awakened and was preparing to get out of bed. I closed my eyes and soon became aware of an unusual feeling, one I'd never experienced before: I truly felt as though I were floating up to the ceiling!

My eyes were shut, but I was very much awake. I even remember thinking, *I can't believe this is happening! I'm actually awake, and I'm experiencing this feeling of floating!* Then I heard some very high-pitched, wavering noises. I felt that they were coming from some sort of higher beings, so I mentally asked them what was going on. Despite their voices not speaking actual English, I intuitively felt the answer: *You are safe.*

Finally, I opened my eyes. I was on my bed, and the feeling slowly subsided. I then fell into sleep again. In my dream, a dark-skinned man in a white suit approached me. He told me that the coming year would bring a big change, but that he'd be there to help me.

As he started to leave, I asked him his name. He continued to depart, but then I heard: "Michael."

When I awoke, I raced out of bed to tell my mom what had happened. She was really excited. "Maybe he was talking about a career change!" she said.

"Hopefully," I answered, yet deep within me, I felt that Michael's offer of help would somehow have to do with something more tragic.

A few months later, my wonderful mother was diagnosed with leukemia, and she passed away. I was devastated, as she was one of my best friends. Soon after, I moved out of her place, got married, and bought a home with my husband: really big changes, as Archangel Michael told me about in my dream. And I did feel as though I was being helped, like I was being buoyed up along the way.

Many people have told me that they have dream visitations to prepare them for major life changes, as Emma Lee experienced. She was comforted by knowing that Michael was with her, keeping her safe throughout her mother's passing and into her new married life. The archangel is always with us, through every pleasant and every painful experience. Yet when life is stressful, our senses dull and we may not feel his presence as strongly. That's one reason why Michael makes dream appearances to help those who are upset, since the mind is quieter during sleep.

A woman named Maribel was grateful for her dream visitation from the archangel, which was not only comforting, but healing as well. As you read about her experience, note how she saw Michael's blue light—even in her dream!

When I was a little girl growing up in Lima, Peru, my friends and I played a game named "San Miguel" (St. Michael). By some spontaneous agreement among us, several of the neighborhood kids would split up into two groups, each a mix of girls and boys. One group would volunteer to play the part of the "bad people," and the other took on the role of the "good people."

Then, while the good people sat on the sidewalk, acting innocent and saintly, the bad ones would come over to try to take them away— that is, the bad group would begin to drag the good group away. The good people would start shouting out for Archangel Michael, calling loudly: *"San Miguel! San Miguel! San Miguel!"* Then a child posing as Archangel Michael would come out immediately to save the good people.

Since those times, I've always thought of Michael as being present in my life to help me in any dangerous situation.

One time I went through a very bad experience. After praying and crying hard, I fell asleep. I dreamed that I was standing at the entrance to my house, and I looked to the left and there stood Archangel Michael. He was tall, emanating a flood of bluish white light. He seemed very powerful while he was floating above the ground. I started to cry in my dream because his presence

was so strong that it was healing me right in that moment.

I remember this apparition as if it occurred only last night. It was real, and I will never forget it. It's one of the most beautiful blessings I've received from God.

Two years ago, I bought a wonderful statue of Archangel Michael, which is in my bedroom. I love it! He looks so beautiful and powerful! I *do* know that he is with me all the time!

In addition to coming upon Archangel Michael in dreams, many people report seeing him when they're relaxed, such as during a massage or meditation. When we're calm, we're more receptive to the angels. We notice their fine energies and love.

Cathie McCarthy connected with Michael while she was relaxing in bed, but *she* wasn't the one who saw him, as her story reveals:

My boyfriend and I had just moved from the United Kingdom to Arizona. We were staying at a friend's house, and I was feeling displaced, with fears of where my life was going. I lay in bed and silently called upon Archangel Michael. Normally when I do so, I see sparkling purple and blue lights. But that night, although I could feel his presence, I couldn't see his colors.

My boyfriend was silently lying next to me as well, resting after many days of moving and driving. Then all of a sudden, he said to me, "I can see a very tall man at the foot of the bed! He looks like he's Scandinavian or something."

My boyfriend had no idea that I'd just called upon Archangel Michael or what the angel looked like. So I asked him to continue with his description.

He said, "He's about 7'2", with long blond hair, and very muscled."

"Is he wearing strappy sandals?" I asked.

"Yes," my boyfriend replied, and then went on to talk about his outfit. He described Archangel Michael to a T! I was so happy—this was his first time seeing an angel or any spiritual vision!

This experience filled us both with love and promise for our new home in the United States and gave us hope that our lives together would be good, and abundant with caring. We knew we had protection and courage to carry on our journey to find a home and to settle my boys in a school. After seeing Archangel Michael, all things fell into place. We felt guided as to which direction to take, in just a week we found a house to rent, the best schools in the area were only a mile away, and my boyfriend started working.

We thank Archangel Michael daily for all of his love, help, and support.

As Cathie and her boyfriend experienced, when you meet Michael, everything in your life becomes more positive and harmonious. Seeing him is so much more than having a "vision," because the experience is simultaneously healing and comforting.

Many people describe their Michael visitations as being multisensory. They not only see the archangel, but they also feel his physical touch, as well as their own hearts opening with joy and warmth. This was the experience that Sian Williams had when she encountered Archangel Michael during a meditation:

> My whole life, I've felt like there was someone or something with me to help me through the really bad times. My childhood was filled with pain and loss. Yet through it all, I never felt alone, and I always sensed that I had a shoulder to cry on, even if I didn't know *whose* it was.
>
> Then one day I attended an angel workshop. I didn't really want to go because it was my one day off from work. But I went anyway, and I'm very glad that I did because I had one of the best experiences of my life that day.
>
> Everyone at the workshop seemed to know all about angels. *I* didn't know much, but there was such a wonderful feeling in the room. Although it was a cold winter morning outside, it felt *so* warm inside.
>
> During a meditation at the workshop, I met Archangel Michael. He was a beautifully handsome man with a sword. He put his arm around me, and I felt as if he took all my problems away. I started to cry, but they were tears of joy because I finally knew who had been with me my entire life!

Reading through these stories and examples, perhaps you've now realized that you've seen Archangel Michael, his sparkling light, or the signs that he leaves.

But Michael's connection with us is far more than visual. He also communicates through spoken words, especially when someone needs clear guidance in a hurry, as we'll explore in the next chapter.

CHAPTER TWO

HEARING THE VOICE OF MICHAEL

Of all the angels, Michael has the loudest and clearest voice. He's definitely the easiest Divine messenger to hear. He also has a distinctively blunt speaking style. He gets right to the point, but always with love and a sense of humor.

I'm confident that it was Michael's voice that I heard before and during my carjacking experience on July 15, 1995. He told me exactly how to prevent the crime—and then when I didn't listen to his guidance and found myself in the middle of an armed robbery of my car and purse, he instructed me how to escape it unharmed.

During crises, people hear Michael's voice as loudly and clearly as if another person were talking. It's different from the soft inner voice that's sometimes discernible during meditations. When the archangel issues a helpful warning, there's no mistaking his voice for an inner whisper—he's perfectly loud and clear.

From all of the archangel stories I've read and heard, I'd say that people hear Michael's loud voice most often while driving. His loving commands help drivers avoid accidents, and his presence calms everyone in the car. And very often his guidance seems counterintuitive, such as when he tells people to take their hands off of the steering wheel. But always, Michael's guidance is 100 percent accurate and trustworthy, as Janca Lesleigh Cox discovered for herself:

> After nursing my parents through illnesses and saying good-bye to them when they passed, I decided to leave our home and start a new life in another country. So I packed my belongings in a trailer hitched to my car and put my cat, Pippin, in a special cage in the backseat and my little dog, Heidi, on the passenger seat.
>
> Before we began the 2,500-mile drive from Zimbabwe to Cape Town, South Africa, I asked Archangel Michael for protection, guidance, and grace. He had been my firm friend for many years, so I trusted that he would be with me on my grand trek.
>
> In the pouring rain, we started our journey southward from the South African side of the border. I drove each day according to my pets' energy levels and was always guided perfectly to bed-and-breakfasts that accepted animal guests.
>
> The road was very straight and extremely boring through the Karoo Desert's endless scrub. Without a car radio or a CD player, I caught myself nodding off. I then heard a strong male

voice say firmly, "Pull off the road right now!" I obeyed without thinking, just seconds before a Mack truck barreled past me in the middle of the road, where it had been straddling the white dividing line!

It's been a year since we made that five-day epic journey, and I continually sense that I'm guided and nudged by my angels and the archangels. I feel truly blessed that Michael showed himself so prominently when I needed him most.

Janca retained her free will to choose whether to follow Michael's guidance to "pull off the road." Fortunately, most of us willingly adhere to the archangel's urgent messages. In a crisis, his pitch and tone are similar to a surgeon demanding a scalpel from a nurse. He's not trying to be bossy or bark orders at us; rather, he just wants to get our attention and put us into action mode. The archangel always sounds loving and compassionate while he's commanding us to take lifesaving action.

Sometimes Michael's urgent messages seem illogical or unfeasible. One of my favorite stories on this topic comes from a woman named Sue—who, fortunately, followed the archangel's guidance. Her decision to trust him proved lifesaving for her and her children:

> Many years ago when I was in an abusive marriage, I prayed nightly for God and Archangel Michael to give me the strength to face another day or to find a way to get out. And each day I stayed in the marriage, thinking that my children

should have an intact family and hoping that things would get better.

Then one night as I was praying, I heard a male voice who identified himself as Archangel Michael. He clearly told me that my children were in danger, and that I needed to be strong enough to leave. He explained that it's not the Creator's will for wives to be abused and that my husband's heart was hard and he wouldn't hear God and stop harming me or the children. I didn't believe Michael, though, because up until that time, my husband had only hurt me and hadn't abused our kids.

Two days later when my husband started hitting me, my 13-year-old son, David, ran to the phone to call the police—and my husband went after him and pushed him down a flight of stairs. I then went to dial 911, and my husband ran outside and pulled out the phone wires from where they attach to the house.

I rushed over to David, who was badly bruised. He told me that he'd seen wings as he was falling that had cushioned his blow and prevented him from breaking his neck. The angels were keeping us safe throughout this nightmare!

Still, I needed more help that night, as we lived in a very rural area where the closest neighbor was five miles away, and my husband had taken away my car keys. So I started praying. Archangel Michael came to me again and said, "Go outside and reattach the wires and call the police."

I don't know anything about telephone wiring, but I obeyed . . . and it was like I was a phone-line technician. Miraculously, I knew just what to do—it was definitely heavenly intervention. I called the police, who took me and the children to a women's shelter. They found my husband and put him in jail.

Archangel Michael was certainly my Divine protector that night. I'm forever grateful to him for his care through that ordeal, and I credit him with our safety.

Some years later, I was divorced and had no desire to be with anyone else after my painful marriage. But when I met a man who told me that Michael was his patron angel, I knew that I had to give him a chance.

We've been together four years now, and my new husband is like Archangel Michael in so many ways—he's incredibly protective and caring toward me and my children. Through all of this, I began to study angels, and now I listen to them rather than thinking that I know better.

When Michael issues a warning, he always gives us guidance and direction. He never makes frightening statements, but instead offers action steps. And sometimes, as Carolyn Skalnek discovered, he only needs to say a single word:

It started out just like any other night but ended amazingly. The kids were tucked in, and now it was my turn to retire. I wandered through

the house toward the bedroom, turning off lights and checking doors. My husband was fast asleep, so I quietly slipped into bed.

As I lay there, quite tired from my day, I said my prayers and asked God and Archangel Michael to protect my family, home, community, and world. I fell asleep very quickly and remained that way until something woke me.

Puzzled and confused, I sat up in bed trying to figure out why I'd woken up. I quickly drifted back to sleep, but it wasn't very long before I heard a noise, as if something was hitting the window. It sounded like our pine tree's branches, but that was impossible because there was no wind that night. I listened for a few minutes to see if it would happen again.

I was getting frustrated by not being able to sleep. I pulled the covers up and got comfortable, and I drifted back to sleep . . . until I heard the sound again. And again! Something or someone was hitting the window hard enough to make a thumping sound. This time I was completely awake and decided to rouse my husband.

There was no repeat of the noise as we both sat up and listened, but what I did pick up on was startling: Just as I heard a familiar-sounding clicking coming from another room, the word *dryer* popped into my mind.

As fast as I could, I went to the laundry room. Entering it, I remembered that I'd turned the dryer on that afternoon! The load of towels inside was untouchable, as they'd been tumbling on high for 12 hours. My face was burning from the heat coming out the door.

I believe it wouldn't have been long before the machine caught on fire. My son's bedroom is directly above the laundry room. As my thoughts raced to the stories of people whose dryers had caused their houses to catch on fire, I thanked God and Archangel Michael that *this* story had ended happily.

Thank you, Archangel Michael! *I do believe!* I will continue to ask for protection, guidance, and love.

Reassurance from Michael

Michael's guidance isn't always about protecting us from danger. Quite often, his audible messages instill hope and faith just when we need reassurance the most. John Roche's message from Michael helped him hang on during a serious illness. The comforting knowledge that the archangel was with him may have allowed him to recover. John recalls:

When I was a child, my parents taught me to call upon Archangel Michael. This practice has stayed with me into adulthood. When I was 18, I developed cancer. I went a while before going to my physician to get the symptoms checked out and identified; thus, I had dangerous levels of cancer when it was finally detected.

I underwent heavy doses of chemotherapy on and off for three years, going into remission and then relapsing twice. The chemo (as anyone who has ever gone through it will tell you) was very debilitating. When I relapsed again for the third time, my oncologist told me one day that I would have to receive a bone-marrow transplant, which meant more time in the hospital, surgery, and additional intense chemotherapy. Needless to say, I was quite upset by this and wondered if this time I was going to come through it.

When the time eventually came for the transplant, I had to undergo the most severe form of chemotherapy that the hospital could give me. I spent three days violently ill while the chemo attacked everything in my body. It was then time for me to go into the isolation unit, where I was to spend three weeks on my own, cut off from the outside world. I was feeling extremely low, lonely, and afraid at this point, despite the best efforts of my wonderful parents to cheer me up.

The tiny isolation-unit room measured no more than eight feet by eight feet, and most of that was taken up by the bed and medical instruments. I wondered how I was going to be able to cope with being locked away in this little room for weeks on my own. I felt quite despondent, and through the tears that were rolling down my face, I cried out for Archangel Michael to help me.

In that instant, I felt a sense of serenity and the deepest love that I've ever experienced in this lifetime. A voice in my head whispered softly, "Everything is all right. You don't have to worry about anything. I'm here to look after you."

A knowing and a certainty that this was indeed the case just filled me entirely. All my fears and the darkness of despair that had gripped me a moment before were gone. Tears continued to roll down my cheeks, but now they were of love— I knew I was being cared for. I knew Archangel Michael was right there with me. Even though I didn't see anything, it didn't matter, as I was sure that the archangel was protecting me and looking after me.

The serenity, love, and certainty that Michael blessed me with that day stayed with me right up to the moment I left the isolation ward three weeks later. I had no complications and no setbacks during my surgery and subsequent recovery. Every part of my being *knows* that this is all because of Archangel Michael.

Now I'm in my 30s, and I call upon Michael for all kinds of help. He truly is my best friend, and I still feel his energy and love around me constantly.

You can ask Michael for a comforting message simply by thinking or speaking your request. It doesn't matter what method or phrasing you use as long as you let him know what you need. Some, like John, may hear the words. But perhaps—as explored in other chapters— you'll see or feel Michael's answer. You may even receive his message through another person.

Regardless, the archangel will let you know that he's there, which in itself is a very reassuring message.

Michael the Patron

Michael, like God and all of the angels, is unlimited in his ability to help us. He's perfectly tapped into the mesmerizing and infinite creativity of the Divine intelligence. So, his solutions are as unpredictable as they are perfectly tailored to each situation.

The following story, relayed to me by Jerome Stefaniak, displays both Michael's creativity and his sense of humor:

> Before I travel, I invoke the angels with this prayer that I made up: *Dear angels, protect me and my car as I drive today. Bless every person and every car that is on the road today. And help all of us reach our destinations quickly, safely, easily, and happily.*
>
> I was driving from Houston to New Braunfels, speeding down the I-10 freeway, when I noticed a car tailgating me and flashing his lights for me to get over. Instead of taking a breath and moving, my competitive ego kicked in. The music was loud and riveting, and I was determined that this car *was not* getting ahead of me.
>
> The car switched into the other lane, passed me on the right, and then cut in front of me, heedless of my horn and the fact that we could very well be involved in a crash.

Just then, above the honking and the music, I heard the loud and unmistakable sound of a police siren right behind us.

Oh, jeez! I thought as I quickly slowed down. The other car continued to speed ahead of me. I looked in my rearview mirror: There was no highway-patrol car anywhere in sight.

I remembered that Michael is the patron saint of police officers, so I wasn't surprised that he used the most effective method to help me get back to my right mind. After that incident, I drive a lot more safely!

So how did Michael create the siren sound that caused Jerome to slow down? Did he do so only in Jerome's mind? If there had been passengers in his car, would they have also heard it? These are the mysteries of Michael that we may never understand, but which benefit all of us nonetheless.

Jerome believed that the archangel created the siren sound because he is the patron saint of police officers and military personnel. Michael protects, guides, and lends courage to the uniformed men and women of the world. And sometimes, he helps when *we* are the ones dealing with police officers, as Beverly Wahl discovered:

One evening I went to visit my mom, who was in a hospital in San Diego. On the way back to Orange County, I got hopelessly lost and started making erratic turns, trying frantically to find the highway.

That's when a police officer came out of

nowhere and flashed his lights, indicating that he wanted me to pull over. As soon as I saw the lights, I asked Archangel Michael what to do. I clearly heard him tell me: "Say you are sorry, and inform the officer that you are lost and need help."

When the officer approached my car window, he asked why I'd been driving that way. He was very stern and wanted to see my license. As Michael had instructed, I said that I was sorry and that I was lost and needed help.

The officer became *very* compassionate and didn't give me a ticket. He also helped me find my way to the highway and even blocked traffic so that I could turn around safely.

Wow! Thank you, Archangel Michael! I always believed in the power of angels, but this was a personal confirmation that no one could deny.

Since Michael works intimately with police officers, he can guide you as to the best way to talk to a member of law enforcement. Notice that Beverly received her help from the archangel *after* she requested his assistance. This is such an important point to remember: As I've mentioned, Michael can only help us if we ask, because he's not allowed to interfere with our free will.

The Softer Side of Michael's Voice

If Michael needs to get our attention in a hurry, his voice booms with unmistakable clarity. Yet, he can also be soft-spoken when it's called for. Carolyn Kellis Reed didn't even hear Michael's voice until after he'd saved her from a car accident by defying the laws of physics:

I was driving with my three small children on a two-lane country road near my home. There were five or six car lengths between me and the vehicle in front of me, and we were traveling at about 45 miles per hour.

On the side of the road, a small sedan was preparing to pull out into traffic. I checked my rearview mirror and noted that there were no vehicles behind me, so I assumed that the car would wait until I passed. I was shocked when it pulled out into the road directly in front of me! Since the small car couldn't accelerate quickly, I knew that we would be in a direct collision.

I slammed on my brakes and closed my eyes, expecting to experience a huge impact in that moment. When I opened them (they were shut only briefly), the sedan was several car lengths ahead of me and there had been no collision. In fact, the laws of time and space had been totally bypassed!

I was completely shaken, but I heard a small yet strong voice in my head. It said that he was Archangel Michael and that he'd made the necessary adjustments for me to avoid the accident. When I asked him how, since the crash seemed so certain, he told me that he'd altered the conditions of time and space to keep my children and me safe. We were not meant to be hurt or killed at that time, so he intervened on our behalf.

Since then, I've always called upon Archangel Michael to protect my children and me when we're driving together, and he has done so time and again.

Carolyn's situation called for Michael's direct intervention even though she hadn't asked for help. Her story is an example of the only exception to the "Law of Free Will," because God and the angels do intervene in life-and-death situations if it's not someone's time to go. So Michael protected Carolyn and her three young children by moving the car.

Why doesn't the archangel save everyone from death, then? This is an age-old question that we may never fully understand in this life. My theory is that people have "exit times" when they're predestined to leave the earth. Everyone prearranges these times in conjunction with God's ultimate plan. Perhaps some people choose a path of suffering because they believe this will gain them soul growth.

Again, these are three-dimensional theories that can't begin to scratch the surface of God's multidimensional universe. But what I do know for sure is that many people's lives are saved because of Divine intervention, and most of the time Archangel Michael is the one involved in the rescue.

Just as in Carolyn's example, Michael's speech occasionally sounds like a gentle inner voice. I believe that he normally talks softly and only gets louder when people aren't listening (such as when they're stressed or frightened). A woman named Melody G. relates a story that shows how she turned into a very good listener, since Michael was able to quietly get her attention:

> I was following a large truck while driving 65 miles per hour on a very busy expressway when I heard an inner voice or feeling telling me to move into the other lane. It urged me to get away from the vehicle in front of me, but I didn't listen.
>
> Suddenly, a big object broke loose from the truck and came hurtling toward my windshield. I quickly asked Archangel Michael to please protect me. The piece landed in the road instead of on my windshield, thank goodness.
>
> Something inside of me said to pull over, and this time I listened to my guidance! There was no real place to park, but I somehow managed to get to the side of the road. That's when all of my tires blew out.
>
> I thanked Michael for protecting me, but I still needed his help with my disabled vehicle. No sooner had I finished asking for assistance than a white truck backed up to help me, and its driver was a true angel. Again, thank you, Archangel Michael, for providing protection.

How do you know for certain that the inner voice is coming from God and the angels? How do you distinguish whether you're imagining it or tell if it's wishful thinking?

Well, the style of true Divine guidance is very different from that of the ego or imagination. Here are some of its defining features:

— **Second-person voice:** True guidance speaks to you in the second person, as if another person is talking to you. So its sentences begin with words that someone would use in conversation with you such as: "You should change lanes right now," or "Go check the air pressure in your tires." The imagination talks in the first person, meaning that its sentences begin with the word *I*, such as "I should change lanes," or "I should check the air pressure."

— **Emphasis on service:** The angels always talk about how to improve a situation or how to make your life healthier or filled with more integrity. The ego always emphasizes how you can get rich quick, be popular, or address some other self-centered concern. (The angels' guidance may cause you to *be* rich and popular, but that comes as a side effect of following it by performing a service or making improvements; it isn't the goal of Divine guidance.)

— **Sense of peace:** When Michael and the other angels talk, their speech is accompanied by a feeling of peace. People who hear the archangel's voice during an emergency always mention its calming effect, which allows them to think and act clearly during the crisis. In contrast, when the ego speaks, you feel a sense of fear, emptiness, edginess, sneakiness, guilt, or some other draining emotion.

— **Ring of truth:** When Michael or the angels speak, their message "clicks" as the truth. Even if what the angels are saying is illogical or intimidating, it still makes intuitive sense. The ego's messages, on the other hand, ring hollow.

Practical Michael Messages

Two other characteristics of Michael's voice are his wonderful sense of humor and his down-to-earth, practical nature. In fact, the archangel's messages are never airy-fairy. They're always grounded in his desire to improve our day-to-day lives, as Marcelle Vlasic discovered when he spoke to her:

I'm a professional deejay, and one day I was getting ready to bring a microphone system to a wedding. It was very important for me to be prompt with my equipment so that the ceremony could begin on time; however, my car wouldn't start, so I called upon Archangel Michael for help.

I said, "Michael, please get my car started right away so that I can get paid for this job and help these people who are getting married."

I immediately heard: "Ring the NRMA," referring to the mobile car-repair service in Sydney, Australia, where I live. I only had 40 minutes to get to the wedding, which was on the other side of town, so I didn't trust this guidance at first. I thought that it would take forever for anyone to reach my house and fix my car. But once again, I heard: "Ring the NRMA."

This time I trusted the message and made the call. Within five minutes, the service drove up, and the mechanic had my car running within another five minutes. He was also so nice, as if he truly were an Earth angel sent by God! I was soon on my way to the wedding, and I got there on time. It truly was "Divine timing"!

So far, I've discussed Michael's visual appearance and the characteristics of his voice and messages. The next chapter will explore the unique physical sensations that people experience when the archangel is around.

CHAPTER THREE

FEELING MICHAEL'S PRESENCE

B ecause Michael is so strong, it makes sense that we can easily feel his presence. I also believe that he wants us to sense when he's with us, because it's so comforting to know that we're protected and watched over by the powerful and loving archangel. So, of course Michael the Miraculous Angel has the ability to make his presence known.

Our skin is a sensitive instrument that instantly detects variations in temperature, changes in air pressure, and electrical signals. Just as you can sense tension or conflict in a room, you can also feel when there's great love and strength, such as Michael's.

People report picking up on the archangel's presence most frequently when they've called upon him for protection . . . and as Caz Greene reports, this brings great feelings of safety and comfort:

In 2003, I was taking Doreen's Angel Intuitive Course in Brisbane, Australia. Doreen guided us to ask Archangel Michael the question "What do you want me to know right now?" I immediately heard him warn me of danger on that night's walk back to my hotel room. Michael told me to be careful and alert and to call upon him for protection.

The rest of the day was so full of activities, though, that I forgot about the message as I walked for 20 minutes alone toward my hotel. As I drew closer to my destination, I noticed a commotion: A drunk man was staggering along the pavement toward me, accosting a couple walking ahead of me. The man was shouting aggressively at them.

I was frightened, and my heart pounded at the realization that the man was headed my way and I was alone. Suddenly, I remembered Michael's warning and called him by name: "Please, Archangel Michael, be near me and protect me from all harm."

I felt a brush against my arm and experienced a surge of warmth and strength. I also felt ten feet taller and three feet wider. The drunk man was coming closer, yelling very loudly. He reached me, and it appeared that he was about to yell in my face and grab me, but his hands seemed to bounce off something about two feet in front of me! The man recoiled with a look of shock on his face before staggering away quietly.

Ever since then, I've told everyone that they can count on Archangel Michael for protection; however, they must also *listen* to his instructions!

So, part of Michael's protection is the sense of safety that we experience when he's present. I don't think he does anything extra to make us feel his strength and warmth. I believe, rather, that his presence is so profoundly powerful and loving that our every nerve ending picks up on the extraordinary radiance of this Divine being.

Many paintings depict Michael holding a shield, which acts as a protective barrier. Michael guards us from all forms of negativity, keeping us safe and helping us *feel* safe. Kate Whorlow could sense the archangel and his shield coming to her rescue when she called upon him:

I was walking home one evening, and as I turned onto my road, I felt someone behind me. Glancing around briefly, I saw that it was a man walking about two feet back. I felt really uncomfortable, as though he were practically *in* my space. So I immediately said under my breath: "Archangel Michael, I need your help *now!* Please walk next to me and protect me on my way home."

Just as I uttered this statement, I felt Archangel Michael immediately by my side, wrapping his wings all around me as a shield. I instantly felt calmer. I kept walking very quickly up the road, hardly daring to look back until I got to my driveway. Then I glanced back down the street: The man was gone.

I thanked Archangel Michael for his help. It may have been a perfectly innocent situation, and perhaps I hadn't been in danger that night. But by calling upon Michael, I received the support and protection I needed in order to feel safe.

Michael embraces us with his large wings, as Kate experienced. Although he can stay with us continuously if we ask him to, we usually don't feel his strong presence until we call upon him during a crisis. This is another area where the archangel absolutely shines: He has the ability to instantly calm nerves and soothe hearts.

His radiant love switches us from the sympathetic nervous system (the uptight and alert fight-or-flight response) to the parasympathetic nervous system (where we're relaxed and think more clearly). Michael helped Karen Forrest stay calm and avoid a collision when a vehicle was headed straight toward her:

> As an officer in the Canadian armed forces, I have no qualms about calling upon Archangel Michael (the patron saint of soldiers) for protection and courage. And I certainly did so when the military was posting me to another base, yet again.
>
> Driving with my husband to the Ottawa airport to fly out to Halifax, Nova Scotia (my newest navy posting), I asked Archangel Michael to protect us during our two-hour drive. Halfway

there, I was going 65 miles per hour when I noticed the van in front of me veer unexpectedly to the road's shoulder. I couldn't understand why it had suddenly pulled off to the side at such a high speed—until I saw a car coming straight at me! The car was dangerously passing a semitrailer truck and heading directly toward me, with both of us driving at 65 miles an hour!

I immediately called upon Archangel Michael for help to keep us all safe. As I started to swerve to the road's dirt shoulder, I heard his calming voice say, "Don't worry, Karen. I have the wheel of your car and will drive for you. You will be safe."

I felt an intense calmness sweep over me (even with a car coming at me head-on) and felt Archangel Michael's presence as he began to safely and miraculously steer my car in the right direction, avoiding the oncoming vehicle and the semitrailer truck that it was passing.

Miraculously, no one was hurt. The driver in front of me safely regained control of his van after veering off onto shoulder. I avoided what was potentially a fatal crash, the car behind me wasn't hit, the semi didn't lose control, and the man who was making the dangerous pass didn't crash or cause an accident!

My husband, Wayne, sitting in the passenger seat, was shocked by how composed I remained while safely maneuvering us out of harm's way. Little did he realize at the time that I had complete trust in Archangel Michael's ability to drive my car!

Thank you, Michael, for keeping us all safe in a very scary, dangerous situation!

Karen described how Michael steered her car to safety, which is an experience that others have reported as well. Many people say that after they called for Heaven's help to avoid an accident, they heard a voice say, "Take your hands off the steering wheel," and then watched in grateful amazement as an unseen pair of hands steered the car out of danger.

While Sheryl Groen wasn't directed to let go of the wheel, she definitely received help from Michael in maneuvering her car across an icy bridge:

I live in central Iowa, where the weather is infamous for changing from moment to moment. We also have a combination of fog and black ice that's extremely treacherous. Black ice is difficult to see, and once you're on top of it, it's too late to slow down.

I commute to work each morning, and I always say an appeal for protection to Archangel Michael. This particular day was overcast and dark, and I was hitting patches of fog every few miles. As I came upon a bridge, I heard a very distinct voice say, "Watch the bridge." I slowed down but didn't observe anything unusual.

As I continued my drive, I noticed that the road's surface was getting wet, so I slowed down again. As I began to approach another bridge, the same words crossed my mind: *Watch the bridge.* This second one was elevated and covered with a thick wall of fog. I couldn't see where the road ended and it began. Even my normal landmarks were concealed by the fog.

Once I was on the bridge, I could see black ice on the surface. Then as I looked up, the fog cleared long enough for me to glimpse a car blocking my lane crossways and another situated against the guardrail. Debris was everywhere, and two people stood between the cars, yelling "Stop! Stop!"

There was nowhere to go, and I knew I wouldn't be able to stop on the ice. I said aloud, "Angels, help me!" Instantly someone took control of my steering wheel and, like a NASCAR professional, piloted my vehicle around the cars, the people, and the debris. A feeling of peace settled over my heart, and I knew I was in very capable hands.

My car didn't skid, and my tires didn't even pick up a shard of glass. The angels maneuvered my vehicle around each obstacle as if they were handling a fine piece of china. And then just as gently, my car floated out of the fog, off the bridge, and back into my original lane—without a scratch on it or me.

Thank you, Archangel Michael. What would I do without you?

This next story also involves a scenario that I frequently hear about. Sometimes Michael doesn't (or can't) prevent a car crash, but he *can* hold us steady so that we're not hurt, as a woman named Liliana experienced:

> I was driving to my office when I was broadsided by a speeding car. My automobile started spinning, but I wasn't afraid for some reason. I just exclaimed, "Please help me!" and then felt as if someone were hugging or holding on to me.
>
> I then crashed into a light post.
>
> When my car stopped, I saw how its entire right side had been pushed in toward the middle, like it was wrapped around me. I was conscious and able to get out by myself. When I saw my totaled vehicle, I was amazed that I'd walked away with only small cuts on my fingers.
>
> Most beautiful of all, the next day when I was showering, I noticed some marks on my shoulders. They looked identical to impressions left by fingertips. I'm sure that it was because God had sent Archangel Michael to protect me. When Michael hugged me so tightly, he left his fingerprints on my body!

The Radiant Heat of Michael

Most paintings of Michael depict bright light radiating from his sword. I believe this is the artists' way of conveying the tremendous amount of heat that this angel conducts. Almost like a solar deity, Michael possesses energy that feels and looks like rays of sunshine.

Consistently, when people have a Michael encounter, they report feeling warmth or heat. Some begin perspiring, and many women have told me that they thought they were having menopausal hot flashes!

Isabelle Hannich even found that Michael's presence warmed her on a chilly morning walk:

> I've heard that you know Archangel Michael is around you if you feel hot suddenly, for no other apparent reason. One morning I was attending an out-of-town conference and decided to take an early walk. It was dark when I left my hotel and headed toward the beach to meditate and watch the sunrise. As soon as I left, I started to wonder if walking alone was such a great idea. So I began asking for Archangel Michael's protection.
>
> By the time I arrived at the beach and kicked off my shoes, I realized that I was hot. I thought that this was rather odd at 5 A.M., as it certainly wasn't warm outside, and it was hardly an exhausting walk. It was then I realized that the heat I felt wasn't the air temperature, but instead was Archangel Michael answering my prayers and was keeping me safe.

Isabelle's story shows Michael's practical side! Yet, most of the time, his role is in safeguarding us and our loved ones. This next story from Belinda V. Herrera shows how the archangel can lead you to safety, if you'll just follow his heat:

I've had many experiences with Archangel Michael, but one in particular still amazes me to this day! I learned from Doreen's work that when Michael is around, you feel a lot of heat. This proved to be very valuable knowledge!

I'd just had the exterior of my house painted. I turned on the floodlights in the evening, not knowing that the painters had left the lights covered with plastic bags. That's when I felt heat around me, which I recognized as Archangel Michael. I was guided to go outside, as if I was following this warmth.

Once there, I kept feeling heat all around me, especially near my right side and right ear. I kept waving my hands and arms and moving toward the area where the temperature was highest. I knew something was wrong because it kept leading me to a certain place. I was a bit confused—I couldn't figure it out. To my surprise, Archangel Michael was edging me toward the brick wall, which felt really hot. The heat was rising to the top, so I looked up.

Well, Michael had guided me to do so in order to see that the plastic bags tied around the floodlights were catching on fire. Smoke was beginning to come out of the bags, which were starting to burn. I knew that Archangel Michael had compelled me to go outside and look up so that I'd notice the bags.

I immediately turned off the lights and removed the bags. While I was doing this, I was crying with so much emotion and gratitude and thanking Michael. If it wasn't for the archangel, my house probably would have caught on fire while my husband and kids and I slept.

This is one experience that I'll never, ever forget. I'm very thankful to the spirit world and Archangel Michael. He always sends his message and makes his presence known, especially in a life-and-death situation. We just have to stop and listen to that inner guidance.

I want to repeat and emphasize Belinda's final point: "We just have to stop and listen to that inner guidance." As much as Michael is able to help, guide, and protect us, we have to meet him halfway by paying attention to the messages that we receive from him through visions, words, and feelings. Always, we know that it's Michael guiding us because of his blue or purple sparkling lights, his to-the-point speaking style, the calming effect he instills, and the heat that he radiates.

In the next chapter, we'll look at the amazing ways in which Michael provides protection, including his ability to bend the physical "laws" of gravity, time, and space.

CHAPTER FOUR

MICHAEL,
THE DIVINE PROTECTOR

More than anything else, Michael is known as the angel who rescues, protects, and safeguards. He's always depicted as a warrior, albeit a very peaceful and loving one. Because I hear and read so many stories of Archangel Michael's miraculous protection, I'm convinced that he's the model for superheroes that writers have used for inspiration!

As you'll read about, Michael can definitely leap tall buildings in a single bound. In fact, this chapter has ample evidence that the archangel is absolutely unlimited in his abilities to help us! That's probably why he constantly reassures us that there's nothing to worry about, for he's here with us, protecting us all.

Michael Bends the Laws of Physics

Since angels don't have physical bodies, they're completely unaffected by gravity, time, and other aspects of physics. Archangel Michael can instantly move an automobile from point A to point B, for example, as well as stop time. He performs this Divine magic when necessary in order to save lives. The stories in this section should allay any doubts about Michael's miraculous presence and abilities.

A woman named Sandra is absolutely certain that her life was spared by the archangel's intervention, because there's no other explanation as to how her out-of-control car could have suddenly changed direction on its own:

My brother, my sister-in-law, and I decided to visit our aunt and uncle at Christmastime. The roads were icy in spots, but we had no idea how treacherous they really were. When we got on the highway, I asked my brother to slow down, but he said he was being careful. We hit some ice and swerved a few times, yet he didn't slow his pace. He prided himself on being a professional truck driver with excellent skills. He could indeed handle the big rigs well, but now we were in a small car.

The next thing I remember, we were spinning across the two lanes on our side of the undivided highway and into those of oncoming traffic. The car was a two-door, and I was in the back. My sister-in-law, who couldn't drive, kept trying to grab the wheel as we continued spinning.

As the car made each revolution, I saw a tractor trailer coming down the hill. We were at the bottom, and with each spin, the truck got closer. I began praying and asking Archangel Michael for protection—and then miraculously, like a flash, our car slid back across the lanes on our side and came to rest in a soft bank of snow.

Thank you, Archangel Michael! The moment we were stopped, I heard that 18-wheeler speed by us, blowing its horn! I'm sure the driver was also shaken, since we all could have been killed. We hit no vehicles, none hit us, and I can't explain how the car could have gotten out of that situation and slid back in the opposite direction, other than with angelic assistance.

As we slowly resumed our drive to our relatives' home, we saw cars in ditches on either side of the highway, as well as a large truck that had gone off the road and fallen into the river. We were very blessed.

I admire Sandra so much for having the presence of mind to pray and ask for Michael's protection during her experience! This story is a wonderful reminder that in the midst of a crisis the best protection is a prayer. It's probably a good idea to develop the habit of prayer *prior* to any emergencies so that it's second nature to say, "Michael, please help me!" instead of cursing the frightening circumstances.

This next story from a woman named Amber reminds me of one of my favorite childhood movies, *The Absent-Minded Professor,* in which Fred MacMurray's character discovers a substance to make his car fly like an airplane:

When my husband became terminally ill, I found spirituality, which included connecting with angels. This connection proved lifesaving!

I was driving along a highway with my daughter, approaching an intersection, when another car veered into our path. There was no way that either vehicle could stop quickly enough to avoid a serious impact. In those few precious seconds that remained, all I could think of was that we were going to be killed. Fearfully, I realized that my husband would die alone without us, but that in death we would all finally be together—my husband, my daughter, and me.

I don't know how much time passed from the moment I knew that there would be a collision to the one in which a truly unbelievable event occurred, but it must have been close to instantaneous. As I mentally prepared for the impact, I suddenly felt my vehicle "fly"—it seemed to be lifted up and somehow kept going safely. This happened very quickly, and I couldn't believe or understand what was taking place.

There was complete silence, almost as though time stood still when this occurred. I became aware of my surroundings again immediately after, and continued to drive down the road home. I've relived this miracle over and over.

I can't say that I saw an angel at the time my daughter and I were "rescued," but I did feel an angelic presence radiating a powerful energy of protective love. I believe that Archangel Michael was with us.

I now know that my husband's death was the transition from Earth to our Infinite Home after a completed life here. At the same time, it was the birth of my spiritual awareness and the beginning of a new journey to find my purpose. My life has been touched by the beauty of angels, who never seem to leave me.

These days as I drive, out of the corner of my eye—or sometimes in my mind's eye—I see three very large angels sitting across the backseat. They seem to be squashed together as though there's not enough room for their wings. The sight is wonderful and touches me every time. In fact, I often can't help laughing, as the vision is quite funny to see. This is the sort of thing that brightens my light of hope for the hereafter, where we'll all join our loved ones again.

Although angels appear to have wings, they don't flap them to fly like a bird. However, they can "fly" in the sense of instantly being present wherever they're needed. And as unlimited nonphysical beings, angels like Michael can be with thousands of people simultaneously. They take bilocating to a whole new level!

So with the angels' gravity-defying skills, stories such as the following from Mary Pulvano shouldn't surprise us. After all, if they can fly, why wouldn't they also be able to lift an automobile and carry it to a new location?

I'd just received my driver's license, and like any young person, I drove a little faster than I should have. One night in particular, I was on my way home, waiting for the light to turn green at a very busy intersection. As soon as it did, I put my foot down and off I went.

What happened next still puzzles me to this day. All I remember is turning onto this busy road, losing control of the car, and crossing to the opposite side. My car was facing all of the oncoming traffic! Other vehicles and a huge tram were heading straight toward me.

I thought I was going to die, so I closed my eyes and said, "Archangel Michael, please help me!"

The next thing I remember is opening my eyes and being amazed by what I saw: My car had somehow bypassed all that traffic, missed the tram, and ended up on the opposite sidewalk! There wasn't even a scratch on it, and fortunately no pedestrians had been walking when it came crashing through.

I believe that Archangel Michael saved me that day because it wasn't my time to go. Today he's always by my side!

In addition to instantly relocating cars and making automobiles fly, Michael can alter the direction of a collision course, as a man named J.L. Williams experienced:

When I'm traveling, I always ask Archangel Michael to protect me. In response to an inner nudging, I called upon him one day while driving as I prepared to pass a semi truck.

No sooner had I finished the prayer than the truck's trailer started to turn over right in front of me! Immediately, it was as if a giant hand grabbed hold of it and set it straight. Because I listened and prayed, I'm here telling you this story today.

Needless to say, I have no doubt whatsoever that Archangel Michael was responsible for protecting me.

When reading J.L.'s story, I can feel his awe at the experience. And as much as Michael's abilities seem supernatural, perhaps he's giving us a glimpse into as-yet-untapped human potential. I would love to see physicists and other scientists study these Michael experiences, since they likely offer clues about levitation and other feats that could benefit us all.

This next story from Jeanna Lejk may make animal lovers cringe; however, please don't worry, as I believe that Archangel Michael not only watched over Jeanna, but also the deer involved. The archangel safeguards animals *and* humans, and with his miraculous abilities, I feel certain that he completely protected the buck:

I enjoy driving on a rural, scenic route during my one-hour commute from work even though my boyfriend and family have worried that it isn't safe. Yet, I always say prayers and ask

Archangel Michael to protect me and my car, so I feel perfectly at ease. This two-lane road has many sharp turns and treacherous cliffs, but I always focus on the view of the trees, pastures, and mountains.

One night I was going about 45 miles per hour down the road, listening to my radio and wondering what I was going to have for dinner. As I approached a sharp turn, a very large buck stood in my path, staring at me. I quickly considered my options: a cliff to my right, and another lane and the mountain to my left. But ultimately, I had no time to react, as it happened so fast—I hit that poor deer, which knocked my car onto loose gravel and toward the cliff!

Suddenly, it felt like someone pushed my vehicle back into my lane. All I can remember is the incredible strength that I sensed. My car was back on the road as if I had never lost control. I prayed that no one else would hit the deer and that the animal would be okay. Even though my car had suffered substantial damage, I was able to drive home. Thank you, Archangel Michael, for your continual presence in our lives!

These stories are reminders that Heaven helps in many creative ways. When asking for assistance, release any concerns about how your prayer will be answered, because the method may be something that completely defies normal logic.

With Michael's Help,
You're Completely Safe and Protected

Michael's miraculous strength and gravity-defying powers aren't limited to maneuvering vehicles. He also protects us by altering, undoing, or blocking the source of our fear. No matter what the situation, Michael can protect us, as Brenda L. Hann discovered:

I live in a Los Angeles apartment building without a garage. One night I was walking from my car to my building when I noticed a huge German shepherd blocking the gated entrance. The dog showed signs of tension as I approached, and his body posture changed into attack mode. His eyes were fixed on me, and his ears were tense, giving him a scary look. This was a pretty large animal with long limbs, and he was probably taller than I am if he stood up on his back legs.

The dog got really upset when I was five feet away. He started growling and barking really aggressively with his ears down. As he was ready to lunge at me, in that moment I mentally called, *Michael!* The next thing that happened was amazing: All sound and action paused, and the dog jumped back from the sidewalk to the street, where he continued to bark like crazy for a moment before finally running away!

I walked to the entrance praying to Michael to keep him away, and as soon as I passed through the gate and closed it, my hands were shaking seriously and my knees were like rubber. I firmly believe that the archangel intervened and got the dog to run away. I went home and lit a candle for Michael in gratitude and in acknowledgment of his presence.

What I love about Brenda's story is that it's a perfect example of how the archangel's help defies normal logic. This is why I continually emphasize that we needn't worry about *how* our prayers will be answered, because Heaven's creativity and power is unlimited. As Brenda discovered, Michael can stop a menacing dog in his tracks.

Perhaps you've had an experience where you called upon the angels while in an airplane. If you haven't yet discovered this, Christine Cowl's story illustrates how Michael and the other heavenly beings make flying safe and smooth:

> I was traveling from Tennessee to New York during a season of very bad storms. The flight was rocky and I was scared, so I called upon Archangel Michael and his Band of Mercy to level out the plane and take us safely to our destination.
>
> Well, the angels really did help us, because we made it into New York's airport safe and sound. My taxicab driver said that he'd been waiting all day for a fare and we were the only plane that had made it into New York. All the others were rerouted to other airports.
>
> I consistently call upon Archangel Michael and his Band of Mercy whenever I'm traveling and the plane ride gets a little scary. As a result, I

always experience complete safety and miracles such as this one.

Archangel Michael *does* help make traveling safe and smoother, and that also includes travel by automobile. I could only hope that you and I would have the same presence of mind to call upon Michael that a woman named Andrea did when her car was stuck in the path of a speeding train:

I was driving over railroad tracks when I heard the sound of a train racing toward me unexpectedly because the crossing arms and warning lights were broken. All of the traffic stopped, and I found myself on the tracks with the train approaching, its lights flashing and horn blowing. The cars in front of and behind me weren't moving, so there was absolutely nowhere for me to go.

I shouted, "Archangel Michael, stop it! Stop it, Michael!" By some miracle, the car in front of me moved forward! I accelerated at the speed of light, feeling the wind of the train flying by my car and shaking it side to side.

My experiences with Archangel Michael are many over the years—always in the car. When I've summoned his help, I've been able to escape unharmed from situations that might have otherwise had fatal endings. And it's all thanks to Michael!

Not only does the archangel assure our safety when we're driving, but he also protects our car and other physical possessions, as Donna Murray experienced herself:

> I've been calling upon Archangel Michael for protection for so long that it's become automatic for me to say his name even for small things. Every time I get into my car, I ask Michael to surround it with his white light of love, power, and protection. I also ask that I hit nothing and no one, and that no one and nothing hit me.
>
> One day my son had a friend over. When his mother came to pick him up, we stood in the driveway for a few minutes talking. She got into her car, and as she started to leave, I realized that she was backing right into *my* car! All I had time to do was say "Michael!" as she backed into it. I stood there and watched her bumper crunch into mine.
>
> She quickly pulled forward, jumped out of her car, and yelled, "Oh my God! What have I done?" But when we looked at the bumpers, there wasn't a dent or a scratch on either one! All I could do was laugh and say, "Thank you, Michael!"

Each of these stories is a wonderful reminder that if we just call upon Michael, he's able to protect us in all ways. We can also ask him to safeguard our loved ones. While the archangel can't force his help onto someone who doesn't want it, his presence can provide a protective barrier and guiding force. In the following story,

Lynne Martin recalls how she asked Michael to protect her son:

> I call upon Archangel Michael daily for his loving protection of my family and me, since we live in South Africa, a country where crime is a way of life. My teenage children want to go out at night to clubs, and I can't describe the horror stories that we hear on a regular basis. That's why I count so heavily on St. Michael's invaluable help . . . and he's never let me down.
>
> My son usually returns from the clubs around 2 A.M. Always, without fail, something wakes me up 30 minutes before he arrives, and I automatically thank Archangel Michael for protecting my child.
>
> One such night, I didn't wake up, and when dawn broke around 5, I panicked, uncertain as to my son's safety and whereabouts. I ran to his room and saw that he wasn't home. I tried to phone him on his cell, but there was no response. So I sat down, took a deep breath, and told myself to relax and speak to Archangel Michael. I said to him, "Oh, my beloved Michael, only you can help me now. I know that you're looking after my child, and I trust you, so please let me know he's okay."
>
> Within three minutes flat, my son phoned and told me that he'd had to take a few friends home and had slept over but would soon be home. My first thought was: *Oh, thank you, Michael! I love you!*

I believe that Michael guided Lynne's son to call her. Only the strength of the archangel could get through to a busy teenage boy and remind him to call his mother! I also believe that the prayers that Lynne says 30 minutes before her son comes home each night keep him safe after he leaves the club.

The following story from Tania Rome also illustrates that we can ask Archangel Michael to help others:

> A few months ago, my boyfriend, Arran, had his bike stolen from outside our apartment in the middle of the night. The person who took it cut through a thick bike chain, and we were surprised that they did this so quietly. A lot of bikes get stolen where we live, and it's rare for people to get them back.
>
> As soon as my boyfriend told me the bike was gone, I asked Archangel Michael to return it immediately and undamaged. To Arran's amazement, the police called three hours later to say they'd found his bike. It had been abandoned in a car park, with no damage.
>
> The people I've told this story to have been impressed or have commented that it's unusual or very lucky. I can't tell them all that I asked Archangel Michael to help, because not everyone believes in such things, but *I* quietly know that luck didn't have anything to do with it.

Tania's story is another example of how Michael is a champion of justice and fairness. Because he's an upholder of truth, he's protective of those who are unfairly accused, as Maura Canty discovered when the archangel provided legal safeguarding for her:

I've been studying metaphysics for many years and have worked a little bit with angels. Before I had my experience with Michael, I had a hard time asking angels for support because: (1) I wasn't really sure they were there, (2) I have difficulty asking *anyone* for help, and (3) I didn't really think I should be troubling Heaven with my problems or requesting assistance in any way. Yet when I needed the angels in a way I never had before, I truly believe that Michael protected me.

I work in the mortgage industry as a loan officer. Years ago I was employed by a company and had an assistant who worked for me originating home loans. I was very busy, and I had little time to pay attention to what my assistant was doing. I had no idea that she was committing fraud under my nose!

One day I received a call from the State Bureau of Investigation, who said that I was to present myself to a grand jury for indictment on fraud against the government. I was horrified! I knew I'd done nothing wrong, so I contacted a lawyer, who learned that the case against me was strong. An investigator informed him that I would definitely be indicted.

So I hired the top attorney in the field. He, too, said the same thing: "Tell your family and make arrangements for your son, because you will be indicted for sure. Then we'll have to fight them—at a cost of $30,000." The attorney explained that if we lost, I'd be in prison for five to eight years!

I was innocent and I knew it, yet I was spinning out of control. Thankfully, that's when I remembered the angels.

I called upon Archangel Michael, lit blue candles in his honor (since that's the color he's associated with), and asked him to enfold me in his wings and protect me from false accusations and let the truth be known. Every day, I invoked Archangel Michael to surround me and protect me. I sent my son to live with family members while I waited to be arrested. It was a horrible time, but I believed that Michael would protect me and the truth would come to light.

Well, my faith was rewarded! My attorney and all parties concerned were shocked when I wasn't indicted. They said that this investigator had been so positive he had a case against me without a doubt. Time passed, the grand jury was dismissed, and I was never called in or arrested. My name was kept out of the whole scandal as well. My old assistant was indicted, though, and she's currently serving time.

All I can say is that I know Archangel Michael saved my life. He protected me and my son, whose name is also Michael. It reinforced my belief in the angelic realm, and ever since then, I tell everyone about the messengers from Heaven and my experiences with them. Thank you, Archangel Michael!

Michael is always with us, continually watching over everyone and the entire planet. As I've mentioned several times, he's unlimited in his ability to be with us all simultaneously and to provide unique, individualized attention to anyone who asks.

In the next chapter, we'll examine Michael's miraculous ability to provide help in the form of people . . . and sometimes, the archangel appears in human form himself.

CHAPTER FIVE

HUMAN HELP FROM MICHAEL

Sometimes it's not enough for Michael to swoop into a situation and invisibly fix it. There are occasions when help on the ground is necessary, and in this chapter, you'll read about two types of human heavenly intervention. The first is where Michael sends mortal people in answer to prayers for help, and the second category is where the archangel apparently takes on human form himself. He appears from out of nowhere to provide extraordinary assistance and then disappears without a trace.

Michael Sends Mortals to Help

If you've ever had an impulse to come to the aid of a stranger, you may have unknowingly been a temporary member of Archangel Michael's band of helping angels. The infinite wisdom that directs all beings of Heaven, including Michael, has instant and ingenious solutions to all prayers. Sometimes those answers involve humans coming to the rescue of the person in need. Very often, the rescuers are named Michael, as I experienced when I required Heaven's help during a visit to Adelaide, Australia.

I was doing sit-ups when I felt my back twist the wrong way. I was in pain and knew that a skilled chiropractor could pop it into place quickly. My husband, Steven, and I prayed that we'd be able to find a good chiropractor in Adelaide. It was a scary thought to select one without a personal referral in a strange city and country. "Please, God and angels," I prayed, "help me find someone who will pop my back into place without drugs or x-rays, in one session."

We asked the hotel staff to find a chiropractor who could see me that day. An hour later, the concierge said he was having trouble finding anyone with an opening. Then he pointed to a phone-book listing and said, "There's one more doctor I haven't yet tried. I'll call his office next."

We went to breakfast in the hotel restaurant, and the concierge excitedly came in to tell us the last chiropractor he'd called had just had a cancellation for a 3:30 P.M. appointment. Since I was giving a seminar that evening in Adelaide, the timing was absolutely perfect.

As I dressed for the chiropractic appointment, I worried that it was dangerous to pick someone out of the phone book randomly. Then a peaceful and powerfully reassuring feeling washed over me, and I *knew* with certainty that everything was in God's hands and fully taken care of. I was sure the Divine had arranged for a wonderful chiropractor who'd totally answer my prayers. As we rode in the taxi to the appointment, Steven commented, "I sure hope this guy is good!"

I said, "I know he will be," and I told him about the reassurance I'd received from God.

As we walked through the door of the King William Road Chiropractic office, Steven pointed to the sign and said, "Look at the doctor's name!" The sign read: MICHAEL ANGELI. Archangel Michael had protected me once again by sending me to his namesake.

Dr. Angeli indeed looked like a cherubic incarnated angel, with large brown eyes and a shy smile. When I asked about his last name, he explained that it meant "angels" in Italian. Dr. Angeli gently popped my back into place in one visit, without using drugs or x-rays . . . just as I'd asked for in my prayers!

In the stories that follow, you'll read how prayers were immediately followed up with the appearance of just the right person at the right time. These aren't uncanny coincidences; rather, they're evidence of the presence of God and Michael watching over us all.

The following story from Donna Ogozalek highlights the archangel's connection with police officers and his status as their patron saint. I believe that Michael inspires members of law enforcement to live up to the highest levels of integrity and true service:

My five-year-old daughter, her little friend, and I were sitting inside an ice-cream parlor enjoying our dessert. It was getting dark, and we were the only ones in the store besides the employees behind the counter.

Two teenage boys acting very tough came in and ordered their ice cream. They sat down next to us and seemed to purposely hit the back of my chair. In fact, they did this two separate times. I looked over, and it was clear to me that they meant to hurt us and weren't goofing around. They wouldn't take their eyes off of us and just glared very frighteningly. I heard them say, "We'll get them when they leave."

I was in a panic, looking at my sweet little girls, who had no idea what was going on. How would I get them safely to the car and buckled into their car seats? What did the teenagers plan to do? Should I go tell the employees behind the counter?

I decided to ask Archangel Michael to send us protection to get the girls safely home. Within seconds I looked up in disbelief as a police officer walked through the door! I quickly got the girls out of the store. I knew that we had just been saved by God and Archangel Michael, the patron saint of that police officer and others everywhere. Heaven worked to protect us, and I'm very grateful.

I believe that Michael nudged the police officer in the direction of the ice-cream parlor in answer to Donna's prayer for protection.

The archangel must have also anticipated Tina Crandall's prayer, because he made sure that a bear expert was nearby when Tina needed information and help:

I live in Connecticut near a 3,000-acre forest refuge. It's a magical place with a river, ponds, lush woods, and lots of walking trails. There's no hunting, fishing, or camping allowed; and visitors are told to "take nothing but pictures and leave nothing but footprints" on the signs at the entrance gate.

One day I went for a walk in the refuge to connect with the angels and nature. But as I got deep inside it, I started to worry about having an encounter with a bear. You see, my town and the surrounding area is loaded with these animals! They frequently climb into people's backyards. And since it was springtime, fiercely protective mother bears were likely to be with their cubs. In addition, the refuge was nearly devoid of other people that day. I felt very vulnerable as I walked along.

Yet I was also angry that my fear was ruining my otherwise-peaceful walk, so I began to pray. I asked God to please send Archangel Michael to me and protect me. A couple of times I almost turned around because, despite my prayer, I was still paranoid. I then remembered the picture of Archangel Michael's "You Are Safe" card in Doreen's *Archangel Oracle Cards* deck and how the guidebook says that his protection is flawless. I repeated "You are safe" to myself and kept on walking.

A minute later, an older gentleman walked toward me on the path. We stopped to discuss the beauty of the morning. He said that there was a deer a little ways up in the direction I was heading. I commented that I'd love to see a deer, but I was worried about running into a *bear*.

The man explained that he was once the refuge's game warden, and his wife would frequently walk the trails alone and also felt anxious about bears. He then gave me advice on how to avoid a bear encounter and protective measures I could take should I see one! He was so helpful and put my mind at ease!

As he and I walked away in different directions, I was truly relieved to have met him. I stopped dead in my tracks as I realized that Archangel Michael must have put this man in my path. After all, what were the chances of meeting with a former game warden knowledgeable about wildlife behavior just at the time I was getting nervous about bears? I feel truly blessed!

Michael sends human help when we're in stressful situations and can't hear or feel the angels' presence and guidance. As in Tina's story of encountering human assistance while hiking, Vickie Kissel similarly received an answer to her prayer while climbing a mountain:

I'd received many signs that I was supposed to go to Sedona, Arizona, but initially I resisted the idea. Yet I felt as if my soul were dying and I needed a healing pilgrimage to a sacred place, so I finally spent the money for the trip.

I wasn't exactly sure what I was looking for in Sedona, so I began by booking different energy-healing sessions. They all went well, but I still felt that there was something more that I was to learn. On my last day there, my goal was to climb the beautiful towering red mountain known as Bell Rock. I drove to a parking lot near it, not realizing that I was actually in the wrong location for my intended hike.

After 90 minutes of hiking in the 105-degree heat, I was short on water, as well as time before my flight home. But finally, I reached Bell Rock. While my eyes took in the magnificence of this great mountain, they began to fill with tears as I realized that I didn't know how to climb it!

I closed my eyes and sent a message to Archangel Michael: *Michael, help! I can't do this alone, and it means so much to me to be able to climb this mountain!* I opened my eyes and drank in the beauty of the natural wonder before me, while dreading the long, hot hike back to my car in defeat.

Moments later, a man approached me and started talking. He asked if I was planning on climbing Bell Rock. It was all too much, and I blurted out my story—how I was exhausted and didn't even know how to climb!

He listened patiently, then told me that he climbed it at least once a week and inquired if I would like him to help me. At that moment I'd learned my first lesson: Ask the angels for assistance.

Shocked that my prayer had been answered so quickly, I accepted his offer. Usually, I'm very cautious with strangers, especially men. Yet this felt right. I knew that it was safe to trust. This was my second lesson: Learn to trust my intuition.

Walking the path to the mountain's base, I turned and asked the man his name.

"Michael," he replied.

I started laughing, and he asked why. I explained about Archangel Michael and how I'd just asked him for help to climb the mountain. He was intrigued and wanted to know more about the angels. During our ascent, I quickly filled him in on my then-limited knowledge.

As we climbed higher, we began to talk and share more. We reached a point where I couldn't climb to the next level without his assistance. As I took his hand, he raised me up to the ledge. I felt safe knowing that he was with me. Several times I had to stop to rest. Michael didn't mind. "Take as long as you need," he'd say.

Little did he know that I was terrified to climb so far up (or if he did know, he kept the knowledge to himself)! As we rose higher and higher, I'd have to stop to catch my breath and get past my fear. *Archangel Michael,* I silently pleaded, *help me overcome my fear so I can make it to the top.* Peace and assurance would then surround me, and I'd be ready to climb again. Facing my fears gave me the courage to overcome them.

We were about 100 feet from the very top of Bell Rock. At that point it was very hard to climb and much scarier. Looking down, I saw 50-foot drops. I asked Michael to stop, as I just didn't know if I could go on. He was very understanding and said that most people never made it as far as I had, so it would be fine to go back down if I wanted to.

I thought for a minute. I really wanted to make it to the top. Breathing my fear out deeply, once again I called upon Archangel Michael. *Archangel Michael,* I silently said, *I am so frightened! I need help!* I was instantly filled with courage, and a voice softly whispered to me, *You can do this. I am with you—you will not fall!*

Taking another gulping breath before I changed my mind, I told my hiking companion: "Let's rock! We're going to the top!" Minutes later, I stood on top of Bell Rock. My legs were shaking like a newborn colt, and my breathing was harsh. As I looked out over the massive red rock, I knew that I was never alone. With the angels' help, there's nothing too large or small, and every dream is obtainable. You just need to believe.

Although the Michael who took me up the mountain was in physical form, I believe in my heart that each step was gently guided by *Archangel* Michael. I still talk to him often and have called upon him for protection in my healing work. Whenever a friend or client comes to me and says "Help!" I immediately turn to Archangel Michael. He has gently guided me, and I've received many blessings from him and the angelic realm.

Michael also sends "Angel Roadside Assistance" to those who are traveling by automobile, as a woman named Anna discovered:

I was driving home one very windy night when I saw something in the middle of the road. It was too late to avoid hitting it, so the object— a bucket—got stuck under my car and tire. Luckily there wasn't too much traffic, so I got out of my car at the stop sign. I thanked the angels in advance for allowing me to remove the bucket and continue my journey home. When I was unable to dislodge it, however, I decided to pull over on the side of the road and call my father to come help me. I was still praying, and this time I asked Archangel Michael for help. (Although to tell the truth, I was a little peeved that I couldn't remove the bucket myself!)

As I was about to make the phone call to my dad, a van pulled up next to me, and the two men inside asked if I needed help. I said, "Yes, please!" So they jacked up my car and removed the bucket. As they were doing so, I realized that the angels had answered my prayers for help.

While we were putting the tools away, we started chatting. One of the men told me that his name was Abdul, and the other man was his brother, who'd just come to Australia from Lebanon. His name was Michael! He then said that it was Michael who saw me on the side of the road and told Abdul to pull over so they could help me. I profusely thanked them

. . . and, of course, Archangel Michael, and have not doubted his helpful powers since!

In many archangel stories (such as my chiropractor experience and Anna's rescue), the person who miraculously offers assistance is named Michael. Perhaps this is because those who are named for the archangel—calling themselves, for example, Michael, Michelle, Mikael, and so forth—work with him closely.

Stories such as Anna's and the next one from Lisa Grubb are reminders that we're never alone, even when our vehicle is stuck in the middle of nowhere:

> I was in a new relationship with a woman who didn't believe in angels or Divine intervention. Our spiritual differences caused us tension, so we decided to take a vacation to see if we could work through these issues. We found a lovely hotel two hours north of Sydney on the coast, and the owner suggested we take my four-wheel-drive vehicle along the isolated beaches. My partner and I enjoyed the thrill—and some deep conversation along the beach drive. We finally agreed to disagree about our spiritual beliefs.
>
> We followed the road until we saw a sign that said: No BEACH ACCESS. Yet we knew the water was just around the bend. So I drove around the sign and went about 100 meters [300 feet] but soon realized the sand was very deep. I decided to turn around and go back, but my vehicle just sunk farther in. After 20 minutes of very frustrating attempts to get out of the sand, we still kept

sinking deeper. As we sat inside the truck, my partner insisted that I had to go get help.

I took a breath, leaned my head onto the steering wheel, closed my eyes, and out loud asked Archangel Michael to send us help, now! Before my partner could finish questioning "What do you think *that* will do?" I was outside my truck talking to four large men who had suddenly appeared and asked if we needed help.

The men had been running along the beach, in training for the He-Man competition in town, and they worked until they freed my truck from the sand and saw us back up to the main road. It was an amazing blessing . . . because not only did it save me from walking to town to get a tow truck, but it also helped my partner understand why I very much believe in angels!

Michael sends human help when we're traveling, whether by airplane, train, cab, or boat. It's a good idea to ask him to assist you as you prepare for a trip. He can smooth the way while you make plane and hotel reservations and then help you with every step of your journey.

The archangel also rescues stranded travelers, as Gigi Stybr and her husband discovered during their Italian vacation:

It was the last day of our vacation in Italy. My husband and I enjoyed an early dinner in a restaurant in the Via Veneto district of Rome. Our flight back to the U.S. would leave the next morning at 7. This meant an early start, and we asked the reception desk at our hotel to order a taxi that would pick us up at 4:30 A.M. to take us to Fiumicino Airport.

The next morning, we waited with our suitcases outside the hotel. At 4:35 A.M. a black, somewhat shabby-looking car pulled up, and an equally shabby-looking driver got out and put our luggage in the trunk. At that time of the day, not a soul in all of Rome was awake. Even the streetlights were dark.

Soon we noticed that something wasn't right. The engine started to make funny noises, and as we circled around the Colosseum, we realized we were in an illegal taxi that didn't even have a phone. Illegal cab or not, we just wanted to get to the airport on time.

But sure enough, the car stalled and stopped. We were stranded. The driver became very agitated and was only concerned about his broken-down vehicle. The fact that we might miss our flight didn't bother him at all. My husband and I looked around. There wasn't a single car on the road, and all the buildings were dark. Only the stars above us glittered like beautiful diamonds. Far down the street a sign was illuminated that said: HOTEL. I told my husband, "You have to go there and get help." He immediately took off.

I stayed behind on the sidewalk with our two bags. Suddenly I thought, *There has to be another way.* My desperation was rising to the point where I experienced the whole scene in slow motion.

I took a deep breath and screamed internally: *Archangel Michael, please help us <u>now!</u>*

Within five seconds, the headlights of a shiny white car came into sight, and it stopped right by my side. It was also brightly illuminated inside, and the driver rolled down the window. "Do you need a taxi?" The blond, blue-eyed young man got out. He had a beautiful, sweet smile; and there seemed to be an unearthly light around him.

My husband came back a few minutes later. We got into the car, and the young blond man took us to the airport in plenty of time.

Incarnated Angels

The stories in the following section are powerful examples of Michael's miraculous ability to protect us in any situation. He has the power to appear in human form and then disappear without a trace. In some of these accounts, I believe that God and Michael sent an angel who temporarily incarnated into a helpful person.

In the following story from Robyn Holmes, the individual in question showed several identifying characteristics of an incarnated angel:

1. He appeared suddenly, from out of nowhere, in response to a prayer for help.

2. He exhibited extraordinary strength.

3. He disappeared without a trace, before anyone could say thank you.

I was pushing a shopping trolley with a large box containing a prepackaged computer desk out to my car. Once I reached my vehicle, I had difficulty moving the box, as it was so heavy. The box jammed in the cart, which tipped onto two wheels, trapping my knee against the car's tow bar. I'd just had knee-replacement surgery, so I was in real trouble!

I looked around for anyone to help, but there wasn't a soul in the car park. So, since I was in enormous pain, I silently prayed: *Archangel Michael, I need help, and I need it now!*

No sooner had I done so than a voice from behind me said, "You need help now!" and a man picked up the box as if it were a feather and put it in my car. Smiling, he then walked off between two parked cars . . . *only, he never came out the other side!*

I had a clear view and was watching, and I didn't even see him disappear. So I got in my car and said a prayer of thanks to Archangel Michael for his help and his angelic helper. I know there had been no one behind me or anywhere else in sight, because I was looking, believe me. God bless Archangel Michael, who's always there when we call.

The fourth characteristic of incarnated angels that people report is their unusual or exotic appearance. Some people describe them as extremely well dressed, while others have met those who were in rags. Always, though, their clothing or features are unique.

In most paintings and visions of Archangel Michael, he appears blond and tan, with Nordic features. I believe the reason why most people see Michael as blond is because of his glowing golden aura, not because he's aligned with any particular race (especially since he doesn't have a body).

Cheryl Brooks's sister was rescued by just such a blond angel:

> My sister Kathy was driving down the street and accidentally turned into the ditch next to the road. When she tried to go in reverse, the car wouldn't move. She wasn't there long when a huge man with blond hair came to her rescue. He lifted her vehicle right out of the ditch, much to Kathy's amazement!
>
> When she turned to give him her thanks . . . well, he was gone. Kathy never quite said that it was Archangel Michael. That's just what *I* believe.

In the following story from Ann O'Donovan, not only was the rescuing angel a handsome blond man, but he was also named Michael!

> While on holiday in Crete, Greece, I took a two-bus journey to visit friends for dinner, drinks, and a most wonderful evening. At approximately 2:30 A.M., my companions offered to drive me back to the town where I was staying, but I declined,

as they lived two hours away on the other side of the island. I didn't feel that it would be fair to put this extra mileage on them.

After my friends left, I walked to the taxi queue in the town square. The square was normally bustling at all hours, but that night it was deserted and looked like a scene from a cowboy film with tumbleweeds blowing down the main street of a ghost town. The wind was getting stronger, and there wasn't a soul in sight until a little old lady appeared dressed in the traditional Greek black garb. She said, "No taxi?" I replied no, and she then said, "Strike." Well, my heart sank as I thought, *What now?*

I closed my eyes and said, "Darling Archangel Michael, look at my predicament. I'm in a foreign country. Could you please help me get back to Stalis, where I'm staying?" When I opened my eyes, to my utter astonishment, there in front of me was the most beautiful blond man on a motorbike, smiling at me. Now, being single, I thought all my prayers had been answered—and not just the transportation!

I found myself asking the man if he was going to Stalis, and he said, "Yes, I'll take you," as if he'd been waiting for me. He told me his name was Michael.

With all my Irish charm and chatter, I'm a bit shy with men. I had so many emotions going through me, and I thought, *How strange! What are the chances of meeting a blond, Greek Michael, especially in this way?*

It all felt so right. I could *feel* his gentleness—it was so beautiful. We took the coast road, which was well lit up in the moonlight, but what struck me most was the whiteness of my companion's amazingly beautiful hands. He brought me exactly where I needed to go.

As I got off the motorbike, I dropped my bag. When I stood up after retrieving it, the man was gone! He'd simply disappeared! I looked down each road, but he really had vanished. I was upset because I didn't even get to thank him.

It was an incredible experience, one I treasure so much because I believe that he was not of this world! Archangel Michael is my constant friend and companion, and I am so grateful to have his love and support in my life.

A woman named Sita experienced one of the other characteristics often reported during interactions with incarnated angels: She tried to contact the helpful person later on and was unable to locate him. Many times, people are told that no such person even exists! I've received hundreds of stories similar to Sita's:

In August of 2005, my daughter and I, along with three of her friends, were driving from Amherst with to Pugwash, Nova Scotia—a distance of about 30 miles. I'd meant to get gasoline while we were in Amherst, but with all of the fun the girls and I were having, I forgot.

Ten miles before we reached our home, I noticed the "out of gas" indicator was illuminated on my dashboard. We were on a desolate road late in the evening, and the nearest gas station was in Pugwash. I'd also forgotten to bring my cell phone, so I drove until I ran out of gas and then pulled over.

There was nothing else to do but pray! I called out to Archangel Michael and sent pleas for help. Within minutes of my prayer, I saw a construction truck in my rearview mirror. The girls and I jumped out of our car and began waving frantically. Fortunately, the driver stopped, and I noticed that the truck's sign said: NOVA SCOTIA DEPARTMENT OF TRANSPORTATION.

I ran to the driver's side and noticed that the man was elderly and angelic looking. I quickly explained my situation, and he smiled and said, "I have a huge can full of gas in the back of my truck." He poured it into my tank and refused to take any payment. He said, "No, dear, this is a gift from us."

He then urged me to follow as he led us to the nearest gas station. I thanked Archangel Michael and the man profusely, and we drove home safely.

The next day I stopped by the transportation department to thank our rescuer again. To my shock, they said that the man I described had retired and that none of their trucks had been out at that time in the evening.

I thanked Michael again for this miracle! I always send a blessing as I pass by the transportation department, and I still get goose bumps whenever I go through the area where I was rescued by an angel!

The following story from an Angel Therapy Practitioner® (ATP) named Nan Penn shows how Archangel Michael can take the form of a helpful voice on the telephone:

I took my car to be serviced at the dealer and waited for it to be ready. The body-shop attendant pulled the car around to where I was standing and left the motor running. I got in, put it in gear, and drove back to Scottsdale—an hour's drive in heavy traffic. I stopped to get groceries before returning home. As I turned off the ignition, I was suddenly distraught to realize that my house keys and key ring were missing. Only the car key was in the ignition.

I looked everywhere for my missing keys—the glove compartment, every nook and cranny in the front seat, and even between the cushions— but they weren't there. It was after 6 o'clock, and I knew the body shop was closed. Even if my keys were there and I was able to retrieve them that evening, it would mean up to a two-hour-round-trip drive, and I was fatigued and hungry. Yet if I didn't get my keys, I'd have to hire a locksmith to get into my condominium.

I asked the angels for assistance and phoned the auto dealer. The switchboard operator said that the body shop was closed for the night. I asked to talk with someone in the showroom, but the two salespeople said they couldn't help, and their manager was away for the evening.

At this point, I was getting desperate! "Isn't there anyone else I can talk to?" I inquired frantically. The woman on the phone said that there was one other person who might help.

The next thing I knew, a very pleasant male voice said, "This is Michael. May I help you?" I told him my circumstances, and he said he'd go to the body shop and try to find my keys. As I waited for him to return, the significance of his name registered, and I begged Archangel Michael, "Please help your namesake find my keys!"

Before long, Michael came back to the phone and said, "Your keys are in your car!"

"But I've looked everywhere!" I replied.

"Your keys are in your car!" he said again.

"I don't know how they could be. I've looked every possible place," I told him.

"Did you hear what I said?" He repeated in a louder tone, "Your keys are in your car!" I looked down at my handbag and moved it. My keys were there! So, had they been there all along and I'd just overlooked them, despite my thorough searching? Or did they magically get transported to my car?

All I know is that a miracle occurred, and I was free to go home without driving back to the car dealer's or hiring a locksmith. I thanked Archangel Michael and God in earnest for answering my prayers—and also for reminding me to always detach my house keys and keep them in my possession before leaving my car to be serviced. That was an angel lesson with a happy ending!

From their heavenly vantage point, the angels can see the locations of our lost objects, and Archangel Michael made sure that Nan's telephone call was transferred to *him* so that he could direct her to her car keys. Her story is a reminder that we're watched over at all times.

Archangel Michael clearly helps many people live safer and healthier lives through his Divine intervention. My prayer is that you'll recollect this fact if you're ever faced with a frightening situation, and you'll remember— like those in the stories—to call upon Archangel Michael for assistance.

In the next chapter, we'll look at another way in which Michael helps relieve us of stress: by repairing electrical and mechanical items. This little-known subspecialty of the archangel has definitely benefited many people, as you're about to read.

CHAPTER SIX

MR. FIX-IT ARCHANGEL

Archangel Michael is revered for his strength, his courage, and the protection that he gives. Yet, many have also discovered a little-known secondary specialty of Michael's: his incredible ability to fix anything electrical or mechanical. Perhaps this modern form of angelic assistance comes in the face of the new era of technology. Regardless, I probably receive more accounts of Michael assisting with mechanical problems than any other type of angel story!

Archangel Auto Repair

Lest we worry that automotive repair is a trivial waste of Archangel Michael's time or is beneath his dignity, these stories show how such intervention saves lives and restores peace, among other benefits. Clearly, Michael engages in repair as part of his global mission to protect us from fear—the fact that he works so quickly and efficiently is just a bonus, as you'll read.

Since our world depends upon this mode of transportation, Michael performs a lot of repairs on cars. As an unlimited angel, he can help an infinite number of people and automobiles simultaneously, so there's no sense that his repair work takes away from anyone. He joyfully responds to all calls for help, often with his characteristic sense of humor, as Jenny Bryans discovered when her car broke down:

> One of the posts on the battery of my 1999 Honda Accord became corroded, so the car frequently stalled or wouldn't start at all. One day, I was heading out to do some errands when it suddenly died.
>
> I pulled onto a nearby side street and popped my hood. Now, I live in a small town, and normally when someone is stranded on the side of the road, everyone stops. That day, though, *nobody* did. I was passed by several vehicles, and the drivers didn't even seem to see me. I began calling people who might be able to help, but I couldn't reach anyone.
>
> Luckily, this happened right in front of a church, and I went to the office to find some help. Unfortunately, the doors were locked and no one was around. Next, I tried the church's sanctuary. I'd seen people coming out of the building, and there were several cars in the parking lot, so I thought there should be someone around to

give me a jump start. However, I couldn't find a single soul.

I stepped outside into the rain and decided that I had to think of something else. A few weeks before this I had been at Doreen's workshop in Toronto, where she'd taught that Archangel Michael was also known as "Mr. Fix-It."

I called upon him to fix the battery trouble for good. I took a deep breath and walked back to the car. I was guided to sit inside and send energy to the engine. While I was doing so, I saw Michael in my mind's eye standing over my engine. It even looked like he was in overalls while he was working his magic! After a couple of minutes, I felt guided to start the car. The engine turned over without any problems.

I profusely thanked Michael and got ready to finish my errands. I looked over at the church, the name of which I'd never really paid attention to before. The sign read: Sᴛ. Mɪᴄʜᴀᴇʟ's. Smiling at the synchronicity of pulling over by a church with that name, I headed down the road.

The car battery has been problem free since that day. Now, whenever anything acts up mechanically, I ask Archangel Michael to fix it. He's better and cheaper than any other mechanic or technician.

I love the fact that Archangel Michael guided Jenny to his namesake church! He doesn't try to disguise the fact that he's helping us, because part of his healing work is to let us know we're not alone. When we have a profound experience with Michael, there's no doubt as to his reality and power. The role of archangels is to bring Heaven's peace to Earth in whatever way is necessary. Sometimes, that means giving a person's car a jump start, as a woman named Monica recalls:

> One Monday morning, I had to drive to several very important appointments. But when I got into my car, the engine wouldn't start—it was dead! So I closed my eyes and summoned Archangel Michael's help. And as soon as I put the key in the ignition again—*Rrrum!*—the car started immediately!

Archangel Michael is right there to help when someone's car won't start, especially when—as in the case of Helen Demetriou and her son in the following story—it's a question of safety:

> I was driving to my home on the island of Cyprus one winter evening after picking my son up from kindergarten. It started pouring, and the streets flooded within ten minutes. I couldn't see the road through the rain, and there was nowhere to stop, so I had to keep going. I became very afraid and called upon Archangel Michael to be with my son and me and to help us make it home safely. I felt his presence in the car, which made me feel better.
>
> I was scared, but since I could tell that my son was also worried, I controlled myself. As we neared our home, I had to drive through a dip in

the road filled with rainwater. I felt my tires lose traction, and my car began floating aimlessly. Other vehicles next to me were doing the same, and I feared we'd all collide.

I somehow gathered my resolve and decided that I was going to get back safely and that the angels would help me. So I called out in an authoritative voice: "Archangel Michael! Please help me now! Get my son and me home safe—*now!*"

Just then, my car's tires connected with the road, but the engine had cut out. So again I called out: "Archangel Michael! Please start this engine *now!*" . . . and it started! I then felt a huge push, and my car was propelled forward out of the dip and up the hill. The engine died again, but I was close enough to my house for my husband to retrieve us. As we got out of my car and into his, I thanked Michael and the other angels. That's when I looked down and noticed a bunch of feathers floating near the road!

Michael left a calling card—in this case, feathers—so that Helen would know that he was responsible for helping her. Two things are very clear to me after reviewing thousands of similar stories:

1. The angels want to help us live happier, safer, and more peaceful lives.

2. The angels want us to know that they're with us.

Unlike fictional superheroes with cloaked identities, Michael seems to go out of his way to tell us: "It was *I* who rescued you." This is part of God's plan of reassuring us that we're forever and unconditionally loved and cared for. The old beliefs that we must suffer life alone are just that: old. Today, we know that life is a co-creation with the Divine, since we are *part* of the Divine. Just as parents want the best for their children, so does our Creator want what's best for us.

The angels have told me that their chief purpose is to bring peace to Earth, one person at a time. They do so by reducing stress, anger, and fear. They've informed me that it's not the big things in life that cause debilitating stress, but the hundreds of small irritants building up to disrupt our inner peace, as Holly Braschwitz discovered:

> My boyfriend and I were driving from California to Cleveland so that he could move in with my young son and me.
>
> As we began our long drive cross-country, we realized that the taillights on our U-Haul trailer kept shorting out. We would have to pull off the highway and turn the car off and on again several times before the lights would come back on. Whenever we hit a bump in the road, we'd have to repeat the process all over again.
>
> We did this for three hours before I remembered to ask for angelic help. "Archangel Michael, please keep us safe on our journey and keep our trailer lit for our travels," I finally pleaded. The lights didn't go off for the rest of the night. The

next day I again asked Michael to keep the taillights on—and he did!

I know that he kept us safe and protected on our very long journey!

So Michael repairs automobiles as a way of protecting us and other drivers. The archangel's all-encompassing love helps us avoid safety hazards. He also helps relieve the stress of financial worries concerning automobiles, as a woman named Jennene experienced:

Last summer our vehicle started giving us trouble. It was bucking and shifting in strange ways at odd times and inconsistently. My father, a professional mechanic, confirmed that the problem seemed to be the transmission. Well, we were upset, to say the least, because we couldn't afford to have it fixed or to buy a new vehicle. We were in dire straits financially, and we weren't sure what to do.

That's when I remembered hearing Doreen say that Archangel Michael fixes mechanical things. I have faith, so I called upon him and asked that he please help us out and repair our vehicle.

Almost immediately, it began running fine. I felt positive that this was because of Archangel Michael's intervention. However, my husband wanted to make sure, so he took it to the shop on two different occasions. Both times the mechanics said that the transmission was fine and that they couldn't find anything else wrong.

So I told my husband that Archangel Michael had fixed our vehicle for us. He had no other explanation, since everything was running just fine. Now he's much more of a believer!

Michael's intervention boosted Jennene's husband's faith, which is one reason why he helps us in such noticeable and practical ways. The following story from Desiree Heinen also shows the spiritual-healing effect of the archangel's intervention. After she received immediate automobile-repair assistance from Michael, Desiree's faith in God and the angels soared:

On New Year's of 2005, I was driving at about 3 A.M. I was approximately two hours away from home and was contemplating releasing the emotional pain that I'd experienced in 2004. I wanted to heal my heart so that the previous year's negative patterns wouldn't follow me into the new one. I was driving; crying; and feeling angry at myself, the universe, and even God and Archangel Michael! I felt abandoned.

I was also tired of the chronic annoyance of my car's check-engine light, which was perpetually on, despite several trips to the dealer. I'd learned to live with its amber glow mocking me, but that night my anger came to the surface!

So, on that New Year's morning as I was driving and venting, I looked down at my engine light and grew even angrier. I remember yelling at the top of my lungs: "Michael, if you're so powerful, why don't you turn my engine light off?!"

After I did so, I felt ashamed. I was driving on a deserted and lonely highway, and I was disgusted with myself. Then I saw the moon in a way I'd never seen it before . . . it was breathtaking.

As I brought my attention back to my driving, I felt this incredible sense of peace just pour over me. When I glanced down, my engine light was no longer on! After a year of this annoying amber light illuminating my dashboard, it was off. I was in shock, so I pulled over and just sat there staring at it, knowing that at any moment it would go back on. It didn't. I began to sob, and between crying and laughing, I thanked Michael. I apologized for my abrupt words and told him that he rocked!

My life changed from that moment on. The year 2005 was a incredible period of growth, and I worked through every issue with guidance from God and my angels. With the help of Michael, I surrendered my negative ways of thinking and reacting to life. I now truly walk with God. I thank Heaven and my angels every day for everything; and Michael never leaves my side—*ever.*

Electronic Repairs

God and the angels are limitless beings, so they're able to help each and every person simultaneously. I mention this because occasionally people misunderstand the topic about to be discussed. They argue that it's not right for us to ask angels to do our bidding, as they have more important things to do. These tend to be the same folks who believe that our Creator wants us to suffer. Yet, when I ask God and the angels about this, I always hear assurances of their unlimited love and availability. They want us to be peaceful and happy, just as any loving parents would hope for their offspring.

So when we ask Archangel Michael to fix an electronic device or home appliance, it's part of God's plan of peace. After all, how does it affect you (and the people around you) when you're upset because a gadget doesn't work? Wouldn't the world be more peaceful if that type of stress were reduced or eliminated? This is why Michael is so adept at helping all of us have more harmonious lives . . . including in our relationship with electronics, which have become such an embedded part of everyday life.

The following two stories reveal how Archangel Michael resuscitated two electronic devices that were immersed in water. If you've ever had the experience of dealing with a drenched gadget, you know that this usually spells its demise. . . . That is, unless you call upon Archangel Michael for help, as LeAnn Harmon did:

> Money was tight, so when I accidentally dropped my cell phone into a cup of water, I cringed and immediately said, "Archangel Michael, please fix my phone. I just can't afford to buy a new one. I'd be so grateful if you could do this."
>
> I tried the phone, but it didn't turn on, so I called the wireless-service company. When I asked the agent whether the phone would ever work again, the guy just laughed and offered me

a really good deal on a new one. But I truly just needed mine to work so that I wouldn't lose all the stored numbers.

I had an intuitive feeling that I should go ahead and plug the phone into the charger as I usually do at night. The next morning I woke up and the phone was working just fine! It's been six weeks, and it's still functioning great! I know I have Archangel Michael to thank for it—and everything else that turned in my favor that day!

As with LeAnn, the following story shows how Michael rescued a drenched electronic gadget. When Ana Cristina Brazeta's son jumped into the swimming pool with his iPod, everyone assumed that it was a goner—everyone, that is, except for Ana, who had the faith to ask for Michael's help. This story is another example of how the archangel assisted because people's emotions were involved, not because of material desires:

My 15-year-old son, Pedro, dove into our pool with his new iPod in his pocket. Naturally, it got wet and no longer worked. Its screen was filled with condensation.

Pedro was worried and sad, and he tried to get rid of the water with a blow-dryer. But it was impossible to do anything more, because we couldn't open the portable music player to dry out its interior.

I reminded Pedro about Archangel Michael, who's great at fixing electrical appliances. I also told him about one of Doreen's published stories in which Michael clears a couple's computer of viruses, and by doing so, restores it. I explained how powerful he is and about his willingness to help everyone as long as we ask for his assistance and have faith that he'll answer us. I said, "For Michael, there are no impossibilities." I suggested that Pedro ask the archangel to fix his iPod.

Pedro went to his bedroom while I, too, asked Michael to help my son and answer his prayer to please fix and restore the drenched device. When Pedro came downstairs about an hour later, he was happy and carefree and showed me his iPod: It worked perfectly, just as it had before the accident, and the screen was humidity free. It was as good as new! I asked Pedro if he'd requested Archangel Michael's help, to which he nodded affirmatively.

To this day, my son's iPod is in perfect condition, and I'm confident that it will continue to work. Pedro now believes in the power of the angelic realm and doesn't give me a skeptical look when I talk about the angels, as he was accustomed to doing before this incident. We both thanked Michael for his Divine intervention, and we love sharing this story with our family and friends.

Just like Ana, Belinda Morby asked Archangel Michael to help *her* son. Notice how Michael's intervention increased Belinda's faith, a sacred result of the archangel's assistance:

My ten-year-old son, Joe, was upset because it seemed that all of his favorite electronic gadgets broke at once. A button on his bedroom's television was broken, and his favorite movie was stuck inside the DVD player. He tried to play another DVD on his computer, but the computer failed, too!

Joe was extremely upset, so I went into my bedroom and asked Archangel Michael to please fix the computer. By the next morning, it was working fine! Encouraged by this success, I asked Michael if he could also repair the television. I admittedly had some doubts because the button was broken. But my uncertainty didn't deter the archangel, as somehow the TV began working again!

I said to Michael, "Thank you . . . thank you so much!"—not just for fixing the computer and TV, but also for increasing my faith tenfold!

If you've ever struggled with a slow computer, then you'll understand the frustration that Kathleen Buchana felt in the following story. She shares:

My computer is getting old and sometimes runs really slowly or gets hung up, so I call upon Archangel Michael to help me and say, "Thank you, thank you, thank you, Michael!" It *never* fails to work!

Having called upon Michael for help with my computer many times myself, I certainly relate to Kathleen's story, as well as to the following one from Armida Miranda:

I work from home, and one day when I logged on to check my e-mail, my computer screen was a mess. I powered down the computer and restarted it, but still nothing. I did this a couple of times, and then I began running all of the antivirus and spyware-removal software. I tried everything I could think of. My computer screen had black and blue stripes all across it. I didn't know what else to do.

I left a message on a computer-savvy friend's voice mail. I also repeatedly called Dell, the manufacturer, for technical support, but each time I was put on hold, and my call ended up being dropped.

Although I tried everything, I wasn't getting anywhere. However, I'd forgotten to do the most important thing: ask my angels for help. I finally turned off the computer, went into another room, and requested Archangel Michael's aid. I asked him to do anything he could, big or small, to fix my computer. I felt happy when I was done praying, as I just knew that Michael was going to help me.

In the morning, I logged on to my computer as if it were just another normal day . . . and—guess what?—it *was!* Archangel Michael was right there, and he let me know that all I had to do was ask. It's so true and so amazing—I just love and appreciate all of his help.

Michael is available to us no matter where we are in the world, as the next story from a woman named

Shanttelle reminds us. She describes how her vacation was salvaged when the archangel fixed her camera:

> I was in Sydney for the day and had to leave the next to return to my home and work in Perth. So I was looking forward to sightseeing and taking photos to share with my family and friends.
>
> I boarded the monorail in Sydney and decided to take some photos from the high vantage point. I flipped the switched on my camera, but it didn't turn on! I waited and tried again . . . nothing. I'd just put in new batteries, so I sat there in disbelief.
>
> All I could think to do was to call upon Archangel Michael and ask him to help the camera work so that I could take as many pictures as I desired that day. I switched it on again, and this time it worked! I was able to capture numerous photos, especially of the beautiful Chinese Garden. Thank you, Archangel Michael!

While some might think that calling upon angels for the sake of electrical appliances is trivial, each story reveals how Michael's intervention brought peace and relief from stress. In the following story from a graduate student named Asfiya Habib, Michael's repair work also saved a college course:

> I am earning my doctorate in pharmacy by attending a school that broadcasts live lectures from professors at a distant university. The lectures are transmitted through phone lines to

seven remote school sites throughout Florida.

One night there were technical difficulties, and the school was working on getting everyone connected. After 30 minutes, though, I began to worry that my 75-minute drive to class would be for nothing.

So I asked Archangel Michael, "Please let this night not be wasted. Please help the technicians get us all connected."

Within five minutes, we were up and running and all the sites were online! It was too short a time span after my prayer for it not to have been the work of Archangel Michael.

While this next story from Kevin Stewart may seem a bit trivial to some, I think it's an adorable example of how Archangel Michael strives to relieve everyday stress:

I was trying to play a DVD one night when it started freezing and the whole system locked up. I'd get enough control back to either eject the DVD or press play, but then it would lock up again. The machine got worse as I continued to try to play my DVD and my partner started fiddling with it, too. I finally remembered Doreen mentioning that Archangel Michael is a mechanic, so I asked him to please fix this machine for me. He did—it immediately worked, as if there was never a problem. And it still works.

I just love Kevin's story, as it also shows that no matter how advanced the technology, the angels are one step ahead of us.

Household Repairs

Our homes give us much more than shelter. They are retreats from outside stressors . . . that is, unless something stressful happens *inside* the home, such as mishaps with plumping, electricity, or heating. That's when it's time to call upon an expert, and there's none better than Archangel Michael.

For the open-minded, it's fun to picture Michael in his service hat and uniform pulling up to your house in a heavenly repair van with a celestial tool kit. He clearly helps us with household needs out of love. His service is his gift to us; and his reward is our peace, joy, and happiness. (Of course, it never hurts to thank him afterward!)

When Cory Silvestri and her husband asked Archangel Michael to help with their plumbing, the results were instantaneous:

> I was listening to one of Doreen's archived shows on Hay House Radio, where she discussed Archangel Michael's ability to fix things, including computers and plumbing. Well, my husband, Jimmy, had been working on our master-bathroom plumbing for about a week. It was one minor frustration after another, and I could feel him getting more and more irritated.
>
> So, I asked Michael to help Jimmy with the latest problem—the left sink in the bathroom. Within 30 minutes, my husband announced, "It's fixed!" I laughed under my breath and congratulated him for his great work.

A few minutes later, though, he came back into the room, totally dismayed, to tell me, "The *right* sink is leaking now." I thought back and realized that I was very specific in asking Michael to fix the left sink. So I requested that he please fix the right one.

My husband was too exhausted to work on the sink any more that night. But when he checked on it the next day, he discovered that it worked! Jimmy asked me whether *I* had fixed it, to which I replied, "Well, not really." I then told him the story of Archangel Michael fixing both sinks.

The beauty of this Archangel Michael intervention was that my husband and I shared it!

Perhaps one of Michael's motivations in helping Cory was to bring her and her husband closer together through their mutual angel experience. Certainly, such Divine intervention is life altering in a positive way. So experiencing it with a spouse would be especially healthy for the couple, as their spiritual growth would have as its foundation the belief in miracles.

In the same way, Michael helped Tracy Griffith enjoy her mornings just a little bit more by fixing her gas pilot light:

We live in a very old house, and for the entire winter our gas pilot light on our heater would go out after about 30 minutes. Because this appliance is old, it's loud when the pilot light is burning, so we shut it off when we go to bed at night.

Relighting it repeatedly in the morning was very frustrating.

Finally, I realized that this was a job for Archangel Michael! So I called upon him out loud: "Please help me light the pilot and *keep* it lit until I turn it off at night."

Ever since, that pilot has stayed on until I turn it off, and if I'm ever having trouble lighting it, I call upon Michael—and *voilà!*

While this next story from a woman named Kathy isn't technically about a household issue, it does involve Michael fixing the lock on a door. I decided to include it in this section because it's a great reminder that the archangel can help us both at home and at a "home away from home":

My husband and I went on vacation earlier this year. Our return flight didn't leave until the late evening, so we had the whole day to bask in the sun. After having a wonderful time, we decided we should head back to our room and get ready to check out and catch our bus to the airport.

When we got there, though, our key card wouldn't work! We tried again and again, and we just couldn't get into our room. When the hotel serviceman arrived, he said that the problem wasn't with our key, but with the card reader. He said he'd be back with his tools.

Just as he left, another couple told us that their lock had broken the day before, and it took three hours to fix! I was completely nervous and angry, as we only had 45 minutes left to pack, check out, and catch our bus. My husband looked to see if any windows or the sliding door were unlocked, but no luck.

Finally, I closed my eyes and asked Archangel Michael to please help us and open the door. I tried the key card another time, without success. My husband left again, and I closed my eyes and asked once more. Nothing. I had many emotions stirring in me at this point, and I was sad, as I thought that no one could hear my pleas for assistance. Then in my mind I said: *Archangel Michael, open this door now!*

Just as I finished that thought, my husband opened the sliding door! When he'd checked it one more time, the latch just flicked up and unlocked. He said that it was weird, but I knew in my heart that Archangel Michael had heard my call and had come to our rescue! The whole way home, I had such a wonderful feeling in my heart, as I knew that the angels were with us, ready to help.

And Then There Are Those Times . . .

Occasionally, Michael doesn't repair the car, fax machine, or other item as we've requested. In these cases, I usually find that he's protecting us. For instance, a woman tries to send an inflammatory e-mail to a co-worker, when her Internet connection suddenly stops working. Or the man who's about to drive drunk finds that his automobile won't start.

Sometimes the archangel purposely breaks items (temporarily, of course) to give us pause until our actions are saner and safer. At other times, he delays his repairs as a way of safeguarding us, as Claire Jennings discovered:

I sell books at expos, festivals, and markets. One time a book festival offered me a spot for a sales stall. But I was concerned that I'd look ridiculous selling new books when everyone else dealt in secondhand, antiquarian, and rare ones. So I panicked and decided that I couldn't attend, even though the invitation came about in a magically synchronistic way.

I hurriedly composed an e-mail stating that I couldn't be a part of the book festival, but in the middle of writing it, the computer froze! I got it working again and continued typing, but it froze again! I tried a third time, with the same results. On this occasion, I couldn't even get the machine to shut down.

I began crying and yelling, "Okay, Archangel Michael, I get it!" I just knew that he was behind my computer freezing, since he was the one who'd guided me to be a seller at the book festival. So I appealed to him: "Please fix the computer, because I need it." And then I left the room to calm down.

When I returned a few minutes later, the computer was fine and didn't need to be rebooted or anything. There was also a big, fluffy feather

sitting next to it that hadn't been there before—
and I knew that it was from Archangel Michael.
The festival was great fun, and I sold more than
$1,500 in books!

All of the paintings depicting Michael holding a
sword while standing over a beast are illustrations of the
archangel conquering villainous fear. He perhaps shines
the brightest when it comes to illuminating the world
with love and peace by eradicating fears, phobias, and
negativity, as we'll explore in the next chapter.

CHAPTER SEVEN

MICHAEL CLEARS AWAY FEARS, PHOBIAS, AND NEGATIVITY

If you ever feel afraid, Archangel Michael can help. He provides protection and safety, instills confidence, and clears away the source of fear. That's because the best antidote for this negative emotion is spiritual, as you'll read in this chapter.

It's a good idea to call upon Michael the moment you feel afraid. You can also ask him to help your children or other loved ones, as Maria Beaudoin did for her son:

> My ten-month-old baby boy is the joy and wonder of my life! I didn't know that motherhood could be this good. One morning he was awakened abruptly by a loud noise outside and started to cry. I knew that he must have been disturbed, as he normally sleeps very well and wakes later.
>
> I asked the angels to help him calm down and go back to sleep, but he continued crying. Finally,

I called upon Archangel Michael (whom I call the "Archangel Problem Solver") to help him settle down. Not even two seconds after I uttered my prayer, my son suddenly became very quiet and went back into a serene, restful sleep! Thank you, Michael!

Sometimes fears become paralyzing to the point where a phobia dictates someone's behavior. No matter what the fear or phobia, though, Michael can bring welcome relief, as Ruth Vejar Ahlroth shares:

I signed up to take a workshop in Los Angeles. That was the easy part. The hard part was that I was terrified of driving by myself. You see, I'm 65 years old, and my husband and daughter had always driven me whenever I needed to go far distances—which (to me) included anywhere more than 30 miles away.

Well, neither my husband nor my daughter could take me to this workshop, so I thought that I'd have to cancel. But on the day that I planned to do so, I was in a bookstore and picked up Doreen Virtue's book *Archangels & Ascended Masters*. I opened it to the section on Archangel Michael and read how he can be called upon to dispel fear. I thought, *Well, what do I have to lose?*

The next day was my workshop. I got in the car, my heart pounding, and started off. I told Michael, "Okay, we're in this together. I'm terrified. Please come and ride to the workshop with me and take away my fear." I could feel the archangel's presence with me all the way to Los Angeles, and my trip was both safe and comfortable. Now I can drive virtually anywhere. What freedom!

So Archangel Michael heals phobias by boosting confidence and courage, as well as by providing real protection and safety. He banishes fears of all varieties, as a woman named Barbara discovered:

I've always been terrified by the wind. So whenever the weather was really gusty outside, I'd take my blankets and pillows downstairs, where I'd sleep on the floor. That way, I was at the point in the house farthest from the wind. But I never could sleep on those nights.

All of that changed, however, when my cousin who's an Angel Therapy Practitioner introduced me to Archangel Michael. She taught me how to call upon him for protection.

So when the next gales were forecast, I closed my eyes and asked Archangel Michael to still the storm and keep me safe in my home. I also asked him to remove my fear. I thanked him for his time and help, and after a few quiet moments in prayer, I closed my talk with him.

The weather did turn nasty and the wind did blow, so I began to feel a little fearful. However, when I went to bed, it was as though I'd stepped into a different world—the one that I had asked for, protected by mighty Archangel Michael himself. My bedroom seemed to be insulated against the wind. It was howling outside, but my room was an oasis of quiet. The feeling of calm was so great that all I could do was cry and thank Michael for the protection he afforded me that night.

I don't fear the wind now as I used to, but I do respect the elements. I don't take my security for granted, either. If the weather forecaster predicts storms, I still ask Archangel Michael for his protection and thank him for it in advance.

Those who've called upon Michael report that their fears and phobias instantly vanish. And as Alexandra Laura Payne experienced, former fears are often replaced with wonderful, calm feelings:

I have a particularly irrational but intense dread of spiders. One night I had a vivid and disturbing dream about being chased by one. I woke abruptly and immediately found myself in a state of paranoia, thinking that there were spiders lurking in the corners of my room. I mentally called for Archangel Michael to help me and at once sensed his strong, calming presence beside me. I could feel him telling me that there was nothing to worry about, and I even saw him drape an indigo-blue cloak over me like a blanket.

I've experienced Michael's protective powers before, but I was amazed by the instantaneous effect this had on me! Within a second all my fears had vanished, replaced by a soothing inner peace. I thanked Michael, and I remember seeing a comforting smile on his face before I fell into a deep and peaceful sleep for the rest of the night.

When I conducted psychotherapy sessions many years ago, I spent a lot of time helping people who had phobias about flying on airplanes. I even conducted one for a news reporter on network television in Nashville, Tennessee. I say this because, having worked with many nervous and phobic airplane passengers, today I handle the situation entirely differently. Where I once used hypnotherapy, today I rely upon the healing power of God and the angels.

A woman named Cristal Marie found that Archangel Michael calmed *her* while flying. Notice how she recognized Michael's help by his signature warm energy:

> I was very afraid of flying in airplanes. On every flight I'd start shaking, my mouth would get dry, my face became pale, and I felt anxious.
>
> I'd call angels and fairies to my side to give me peace and courage to face the situation. With their help, I was definitely calmer during the flights, but whenever the plane shook a bit, all that composure left me. I'd become afraid again, reject the notion of being helped, and believe that the angels and fairies weren't there after all. I'd experience despair, feeling that I was alone and if the plane went down, nobody could help me. It was horrible!
>
> All that changed, though, thanks to Archangel Michael. It happened on a flight from New York

to Santo Domingo when we experienced such strong turbulence that the flight attendants all had to sit—and one of them burst into tears! The plane dipped in free falls until finally the pilot said that we might need to make an emergency landing in Cuba.

As I sat there contemplating my mortality, I called upon Archangel Michael for protection. I guess I was so vulnerable that I finally heard him clearly. He made me realize that I wasn't so much afraid of the airplane crashing, but rather of losing control over everything and everyone in my life.

He showed me how I had this same fear about control at home, at work, and in relationships. I'd become this paranoid woman who didn't trust anyone, not even those who I knew loved me. All my relationships suffered because of this fear of letting people in.

Right then, I resolved to heal this situation! Fear had been controlling my life for far too long. I tried to turn the whole situation over to God and Archangel Michael but bumped head-on into my fear of losing control. So even though I finally understood my anxiety, I felt stuck and unable to heal.

Ironically, another turbulent flight finally brought me to my knees (so to speak) so that I was able to heal through humility. The airplane was flying through a thunder-and-lightning storm that created a whole new level of fear for me. I was finally humbled enough to ask Archangel

Michael to help me release my fears.

Within two seconds, I suddenly felt calm. The plane was still bouncing all over the place, but I experienced absolutely no fear. I even felt silly that I'd been afraid in the first place!

When we landed, the pilot declared that he was surprised by how smooth our arrival had been. It could have been much worse, and the duration of the turbulence had been cut by half of the original estimate. A dense fog at the airport seemed to lift when we landed, and then almost as soon as we touched down, it wrapped itself around the city again, to the point that flights were cancelled that day.

I know Archangel Michael was there because I felt heat engulf me. It was this heat that gave me courage, made me laugh, and helped me feel stronger. I thought it was a miracle.

I still get slightly nervous on flights, but I've realized it's mostly due to my *memory* of fear. Thanks to Archangel Michael, I've never been that afraid again. He not only eliminated my fears and eased what would have been the most traumatic flight of my life, but he also healed me from resentment. He burned away my previous unwillingness to forgive.

Ever since then, everything has been falling into place. My life is now completely different, and I have tons of new friends and have managed to keep the old ones, too. I got a new job that keeps getting better and better, and ironically, my work completely depends on my ability to trust those in charge of me.

I could go on and on about all the various things that have changed for the better and the many more times I've asked Archangel Michael to heal a situation and have received miraculous results, but I believe this just might be one of the, if not *the,* most important.

Sometimes fear and anxiety is so overwhelming that it creates physical effects such as shortness of breath and a racing heart. This condition, known as a panic attack, is also something that Michael can heal, as Jane Turner recalls:

I had my first extremely severe panic attack five years ago at my parents' house after a shopping trip. I literally sank to the floor and couldn't move. My two little girls were terrified. My mother swiftly called an ambulance, and I spent several hours in the hospital. The medical personnel explained panic attacks in detail and how to avoid them in the future.

Two weeks later I was driving over to my parents' home. Before leaving, I'd mentally asked Archangel Michael to accompany me on the 60-mile journey, since I'd read that one of his roles is strengthening faith and courage.

About halfway through the trip, the dreaded panic surfaced again. I put on some music and started singing at the top of my lungs, but I could still feel myself closing down and terror creeping over me. In tears, I loudly and forcefully said, "Michael, please help me!"

Within seconds, I felt calmer and soon was actually laughing out loud because I had a vision of this mighty archangel—sword and shield in hand—standing on the roof of my car, enjoying the ride, with his hair streaming in the wind! He stayed there for the rest of my journey, and I sang along with him and all the angels surrounding me. It was as if I had a whole entourage with me, and I felt so wonderfully calm and happy.

Luckily, a panic attack is a very rare thing for me now, but I still ask Michael to accompany me on long journeys . . . and I know that he does!

Vacuuming Away Fear

One day in 1995 while I was praying, meditating, and talking with Archangel Michael, I had a vision of him holding a portable-vacuum-cleaner-like device. He put the hose through the top of my head and suctioned toxic fear out of my body like a spiritual version of liposuction. My body shuddered as the archangel removed negative energy that I'd absorbed from my own thoughts and those of others. Afterward, I felt lighter, freer, and happier.

I began asking Michael to "vacuum" my clients, and then in 1996, I started teaching others about his vacuuming methods.

I've since found that Archangel Michael's vacuum is a rapid and effective antidote to negative and unhealthy influences. This technique works extremely well with teenagers, particularly in calming down those who act out aggressively.

Gladys E. Alicea was introduced to vacuuming by a graduate of my Angel Therapy Practitioner (ATP) program:

I was having a lot of phobias and fears, so I went to an ATP, who introduced me to Archangel Michael. At the time I was very fearful of everything, and my phobias were controlling me. I was especially afraid of nighttime darkness and was constantly worried that something very bad was going to happen to my physical body. I have no idea where this fear came from, since I'd never experienced anything that would trigger these phobias. I was also afraid that, due to my worry, I was attracting and manifesting a terrible tragedy.

On the other hand, I had this huge desire to help heal the world, but I always felt blocked. I went to the ATP very distraught and troubled. She asked Archangel Michael to vacuum me out, and I left feeling like a new person.

This shift changed the way I felt and acted and even how I looked! Soon after my session, I saw a dear friend who said that there was something different about me and asked if I'd lost weight. I knew that it was the peacefulness she saw in me.

Most of my fears have vanished. Every time I find myself with thoughts stemming from anxiety, I ask Archangel Michael to guide me, and I immediately feel better. My old phobias about the dark are now almost completely gone.

Since Archangel Michael cleared away these

blocks and I opened myself to him, I've had a lot of joy in my life. I've reconnected with friends whom I've missed, and the relationship with my boyfriend has strengthened even more. It's wonderful! Archangel Michael is truly a miraculous gift from God. I look forward to what the future has in store for me—without fear!

In case you're thinking that you need the professional assistance that Gladys received, the next story from Gillian Leahy shows that Michael provides all the help necessary—you only need to ask:

I called upon Archangel Michael for help one night, as I was feeling very down due to events that had occurred in my past. I didn't know who I was anymore, and I had questions that nobody could answer. That night, lying in bed thinking about everything I'd been through in my life, I finally asked Michael for help with my emotions.

The room was dark, but I could suddenly see "energy"—there's no other way to describe it. It felt like a big warm hug from someone, and my heart just opened up. In my mind's eye, I could see Michael and his Band of Mercy helper angels removing darkness from me. It was as if it were just leaving my body. The vision was so clear, as though I could physically see them. The angels came closer, disappeared for a while, and then flew upward. I had the feeling of being filled with light . . . and then it was over.

The next morning I woke up feeling quite energetic, so I told my husband of this healing I'd received. At first he joked about it until he realized how serious I was. Since that night, I've tried etheric cord-cutting on my husband, with great results. I could actually see all the cords coming from his back.

Anytime I feel down, I call upon Michael. I always know he's there when I feel warmth in my heart!

You also can ask Archangel Michael to vacuum homes, offices, and other people (particularly children, as I mentioned earlier), as this next story from Robin Ramos illustrates:

I first learned about the benefit of working with Archangel Michael when I read Doreen's book *The Care and Feeding of Indigo Children*. I fell in love with the vacuuming technique described in the book. I read through it a couple of times until I memorized it almost to the letter! I vacuumed my children's rooms and then proceeded to do the whole house. I also bought a beautiful ceramic plaque with Michael's picture on it that I placed in front of my kids' rooms.

I've become very good at visualizing, and when I use this technique, I immediately see a huge glowing blue light within my mind's eye. I swear sometimes that I also feel as if I'm being wrapped in strong positive energy. I invited Michael to stay with my family permanently, as

Doreen had suggested, and I sense his presence when I think of him.

I noticed immediately that my son Zack sleeps better and has more settled energy whenever I vacuum his room and add my own prayers of help and thanks to Michael. My son Tyler is very in tune to sounds in his room, so much so that they used to keep him awake. Sensing that he felt unsafe, I typed up the invitation for Michael to stay with us and placed it in his bedroom. The results were immediate and wonderful: Tyler stopped hearing noises that kept him awake. It's been five years since I first met Archangel Michael, and I'm thankful for his presence all the time.

I've also requested that Michael go to school with my kids. Periodically, when Zack starts feeling ultrasensitive and bullied, I call upon the archangel to stay with him, and he always comes home with fewer complaints and upsets. On days when I forget to call upon Michael on behalf of my son, I can really notice the difference in how Zack acts when he gets home from school.

My life has become much more enriched and blessed as a result of calling on Michael and all the other angels and guides. It's such an easy thing to do, and the consequences can never do harm to anyone. Quite the opposite: The outcome is a more peaceful, positive, blessed life.

You can vacuum yourself, your loved ones, and your home by asking Archangel Michael and his helping angels for this care. Request that he suction away all lower energies, fear, negative or earthbound entities, or anything else that is toxic. You can also ask him to vacuum fear or darkness out of anyone who's associated with you (to the degree that it affects *your* free will). The moment you ask for this help, it is done.

Cutting Cords to Fear

I learned this next method from watching Archangel Michael during my healing sessions. Whenever I'd ask him to help my clients recover from debilitating fear, he'd use his sword to sever attachments that I could see growing from their bodies. These attachments looked like translucent tubes (similar to surgical tubing).

By conducting many sessions with Michael and asking a lot of questions, I came to understand that these hollow tubes carry energy between my clients and other people (and occasionally physical possessions, if they have attachments arising from fears about losing these items).

The tubes conduct energy between two people. If someone has a tube (called an *etheric cord*) attached to an angry person, this energy tumbles through it and causes pain in the area of the body where it's connected.

Conversely, if that cord or tube is attached to an emotionally needy person, then energy will be drained on the opposite end. The other person will feel exhausted without knowing why, and this tiredness won't respond to normal energy boosters such as rest, caffeine, or exercise.

Are these cords always negative? They are, in the sense that they're built from fear. Whenever a person has a relationship worry such as "I hope you don't leave me," an attachment forms like an etheric leash.

However, there are also silver cords of life and love that are healthy and nonporous. These can never be cut, because they're built of eternal love.

Fear-based cords are nothing to worry or feel ashamed about, as they're quite normal, especially among sensitive people. As you'll read in the following stories, you can easily ask Archangel Michael to cut these cords anytime you feel tired or in pain. It's as simple as thinking the name *Michael* or saying to him: "Please cut any cords of fear from me." You can also ask him to send love to those people to whom you've had the attachment.

A woman named Trina, who had the advantage of natural clairvoyance, helped her daughter when she asked Michael to release the girl from fear:

> My 12-year-old daughter developed a sudden fear of being alone at night, and she complained of feeling "something odd" behind her. She insisted that our golden retriever, Seamus, sleep behind her or else she'd be awake all night.
>
> While we were driving together one evening, she began squirming in her seat. She squeezed all the way down so that her back was on it. I realized that she wasn't just being a dramatic preteen and decided I'd better take a look and see what was there.
>
> I know how to scan with my mind's eye and clairvoyantly identify things of this nature. Still, I was shocked when I saw a *huge* cord stuck to the middle of her back! I called upon Archangel

Michael and asked for his help in removing it, as well as in setting up protection that would remain with her always. I quickly sensed his energy and saw that the cord was gone.

After a few moments, she was able to sit up and said that her back was feeling better. I told her about Archangel Michael and let her know that she could ask for his help if she ever felt like that again. Thanks to the archangel, my daughter feels safe again at night—which, of course, makes me feel better, too.

You don't need to be a clairvoyant to benefit from Michael's help, though. Even if you can't see the cords, you can feel their effect of tiredness, burnout, or physical pain with no logical origin—and then the relief when the cords are cut—as a story from a woman name Tina illustrates:

Three weeks after my baby was born, I was suffering from postpartum depression. My husband bought me Doreen's *Healing with the Angels* book for my birthday, and I'd just started reading it. Before this, I had no real connection to the angels, knowing only that they were in the Bible and were messengers of God.

I came to a part in the book that suggested asking Archangel Michael for help with releasing negative emotions and depression. I remember sitting on the couch, thinking that I'd give it a go—I'd do anything to feel better.

My eyes were shut when I suddenly had a

vision of an angel coming down from above holding a sword, and he then cut cords from me. I was immediately frightened, as I thought he was severing my life cord and had no idea at this point about etheric cords or attachments to others that can drain our emotions.

Nonetheless, that afternoon I felt an enormous weight lifted, and I can honestly say I owe it all to Archangel Michael for relieving my postpartum depression. It was only later, once I started reading more about the angels, that I discovered that Michael carries a sword and releases our burdens. For me, his healing was immediate and miraculous. I now ask Archangel Michael to be with me anytime I feel vulnerable and need protection.

Anyone can call upon Michael and appeal to him to cut cords of fear. It's simply a matter of asking. It's unimportant *how* you do so, and as Barbara Urban discovered, *where* you are is also irrelevant—he responds to every request for assistance:

> I was meditating while soaking in the hot tub, thinking about how I'd really like to connect more deeply with the angels, particularly with Archangel Michael. I was feeling really relaxed.
>
> I asked Michael to please cut any ties of fear and doubt, whether I was aware of them or not. I said, "Archangel Michael, please sever these ties so that I may have the wonderful experience of seeing the angels."

There was silence, and I was staring at the birds and the trees while daydreaming and soaking. Suddenly, I heard this big sound like *"Foop!"* to my right. On the table beside me, a watermelon that I'd set out had been sliced open, and its juices were draining all over my deck!

I saw nothing but knew immediately that Archangel Michael was giving me a sign about severing my fear ties by cutting the watermelon with his sword! I hopped out of the tub, ran to the deck, and jumped up and down yelling, "Thank you! Thank you!"

The melon was cut nearly all the way through, leaving only about an inch and a half on the bottom—I guess Michael didn't wanted it to fall off the table and was making sure I could see the cut. I was so excited. I *know* in my entire being that this was a sign.

I stared at the melon for a bit and realized that Michael was telling me that he had now cut my ties. I didn't see the angels as I'd asked, but I definitely did get a sign from them!

I love the sense of humor that Michael displays in Barbara's story. Since cords are fragments stemming from fear within relationships, they can cloud our sense of humor and happiness. In fact, cords are metaphysical representations of unforgiveness and withheld anger. As every spiritual path and religion teaches, forgiveness opens the path to true healing and happiness. David Welch's story highlights this:

As I was praying about meeting my soul mate, my mind began to think about forgiveness of people who had wronged me. One was a friend of mine back in Florida whom I'd sublet my apartment to while I deployed to Puerto Rico in the Navy. He didn't pay the rent or the utilities, so he was evicted. In retaliation, he trashed my apartment, and I'd never forgiven him for this deed.

I asked Archangel Michael to cut the bad cords to my friend. I immediately felt a huge weight lift. The physical sensation on my back was like a gentle massage—I knew that this was Archangel Michael cutting the cords. I looked over my right shoulder and thanked him for helping me with my forgiveness, and even though I couldn't see him, I heard his voice in my head say simply, *You're welcome, David.* It's amazing how much better I feel after having forgiven. Now I understand why this act is so important.

As David's story illustrates, asking Michael to cut your cords is a wonderful way to prepare for a new relationship. It's also a healthy way to deal with one that is ending, as a woman named Clarity describes:

I was experiencing a lot of emotional turmoil over the end of a relationship. I felt great pain and deep hurt as I thought about my ex-lover. Eventually, I realized that the real problem was within myself.

So I asked Archangel Michael: "Please, kindly cut away the negative cords attached to me." I closed my eyes and recited prayers with heartfelt sincerity because I truly desired to remove this deep pain within me.

When I opened my eyes, I saw colorful sparks of light right in front of me! I couldn't believe my eyes, so I got up from my cushion and peered out the window, suspecting that the neon lights from the supermarket across the street must have shone into my room. But the store was closed.

I instantly felt that it had to be the presence of Archangel Michael. I recalled reading in Doreen's book that colored lights are the auras of archangels and ascended masters.

I am happy to say that thereafter I felt a sense of great peace within me, and I no longer suffered from any unwanted resentment and pain. I do trust and believe in the presence of Archangel Michael and the other beings of Heaven. Thank you, Michael and my lovely angels!

Michael responds immediately to all calls for help, regardless of the form of the request. This next story from a woman named Chrissie shows that he answers prayers for protection by cutting cords during dreams:

When my young son, Jamie, was being bullied at school, he had a dream that Archangel Michael came to see him with his sword. There was a long piece of rope with my son's name at one end and that of the bullying boy at the other. Michael then took his sword and cut the rope in half. Soon after this dream, Jamie was better able to deal with the harassment, and finally it stopped altogether!

I'm certain that Michael enters many of our dreams in similar ways. We may not remember them, but we enjoy the effects, just as Chrissie's son did when the bully left him alone.

Clearing Your Home or Office of Negativity

Since Archangel Michael's chief role and purpose is to eradicate fear from people, places, and the world at large, he's wonderful at clearing the energy in your home or office. Michael ushers earthbound spirits and negativity away, invokes Divine angels in their place, and shields the area from any intrusions.

It's a good idea to ask Archangel Michael to clear the energy of any location where you spend time. As you'll read in the stories in this section, energy clearing has profoundly positive results. All you have to do is ask.

Most people, like Kelly Roper in the following story, ask Michael to clear their homes because they can sense negativity inside:

I'd just moved into my partner's home, which had very dark energy, mostly from his ex-wife's frequent suicide attempts there. The house was also cluttered with junk and painted in dark colors. My friends who visited commented that the place felt unwelcoming and cold. I asked Archangel Michael to clear the house of negativity, and I followed my guidance to paint it in lighter colors.

Now visitors comment on the lovely and inviting feeling that the house emanates! I see blue flashes of light frequently now and always say hello to Michael, thanking him for all of his help.

Notice how, in addition to Kelly herself, visitors perceived the difference in her home's energy. I believe that everyone is sensitive to positive and negative energy within buildings. Some people may not know *why* they like one place over another, yet they can still sense the mood and climate within a room. Children, in particular, are able to feel these energies, as this next story from Sarah Dickson illustrates:

My two-year-old daughter, Sophie, is extremely sensitive to energies invisible to many people, including negative ones, which used to wake her up at night and leave her crying and very upset. As an infant, Sophie would wake with what we thought might be night terrors or bad dreams. When she began speaking, though, I understood that she was being disturbed in her sleep by restless spirits who would communicate with her despite her desire to rest.

So we began saying evening prayers and requesting Archangel Michael's protection throughout the night. We asked that any energy of fear and negativity not enter this house and that Michael stay with us and protect us all night.

From that time forward, Sophie has slept so much more peacefully (and so have her mom and dad!). My daughter sees her angels, and she says Michael's name aloud each night before she puts her head down on the pillow to sleep. He protects us and keeps us safe.

The following story from Mary K. Gee is unusual because the negative energies in her home were actually wreaking havoc. This doesn't happen too frequently, but if it does, Michael is the angel to call, as Mary discovered:

When things in my latest residence started making noise and I felt ill at ease, I didn't panic. However, it wasn't long before objects started breaking and flying off walls. My dogs were cowering, and the phone was ringing with no one at the other end. I called a friend of mine who is a shamanic practitioner, and she visited to find out exactly what the deal was.

She told me that my daughter had brought these lower energies home from her high school. Once the energies were inside, they detached from her to set up housekeeping here.

She advised me to call upon Archangel Michael to exorcise these things from my home. So I chanted his name and asked him to assist me in the clearing. At first I tried to help Michael by visualizing this event myself. But it was too hard a battle, so I ultimately bowed out and let him handle it, which he did with incredible swiftness! The energies never returned. I always call upon

Michael now if I'm afraid, and I've used him to cut cords as well.

Like Mary, a professional angel therapist named Sophia Fairchild needed immediate and extreme help from Archangel Michael to clear away negative energies and earthbound entities from her home:

> Many years ago I bought a ramshackle house on a hill overlooking the ocean. It was badly run-down, but it was the only place I could afford at the time. I suspected something was very wrong with this house when in spite of its beautiful location and low price, nobody else showed any interest in buying it.
>
> Looking back now, I see that it was glaringly obvious what the problem was. At the first and only open house, the few prospective buyers got no farther than the entry hall before the blood drained from their faces. Most of them bolted back to the safety of their cars and sped away. The real estate agent stood well off to the side, meekly pointing out the ocean views and apologizing for the fact that the house had stood empty for some time.
>
> I, too, sensed the cold, clammy atmosphere emanating from the house, but I carefully ventured inside. I tried not to wince at the broken vintage plumbing, holes in graffitied walls, decades-old junk piled up to the rafters in the grim garage, and personal items abandoned in haste, strewn like confetti across the yard. Yet

the lovely ocean view and glimpses of what must have once been a magnificent garden, now lying buried beneath weeds and trash, gave me some confidence that I could make a thing of beauty from this wreck of a house. And besides, this was all I could afford.

At the auction I was the only bidder, except for a man I suspected was a stooge, positioned there by someone to deliberately jack up the price. Fortunately, I called his bluff and was thrilled to secure the house for a sum even lower than I'd expected. It seemed like a miracle to own my own place at last! My son, however, was not so thrilled.

Shortly after we moved into the house, I began to hear strange stories from my nervous neighbors about the previous residents. An old woman who'd survived the Nazi death camps had lived alone there for many years before dying in my bedroom. A tormented soul, she took aimless bus rides crisscrossing the city every day, apparently to get away from someone or something that was always chasing her. It was sad to think that after all she'd been through, she was so frightened of her own home.

The house had then fallen into disrepair through years of neglectful tenants and an absentee landlord who'd bought the property merely for its land value. The last occupants had been a group of occultists who must have enjoyed the parade of ghosts that nightly streamed through that windswept house—until *they* left in a big hurry. Even my cats knew that this house was truly haunted, but I still managed to gloss over that detail.

I enlisted the aid of a well-known feng shui expert to begin work on clearing the house of its dank, cloying energy. He doused the property and pointed out a couple of powerful ley lines that intersected below the house. We hammered copper pipes into the ground across them, hoping this would calm the energy down, and we moved furniture around in my son's bedroom. When the man had done all he could, he left me with a recommendation to call in a specialist to perform an exorcism. *A what?! Okay, an exorcism. But whom do I call?* He didn't know. This wasn't something that could easily be looked up in the yellow pages.

Right then I began firmly telling myself that I had to get a handle on this situation. I simply pushed aside the feeling that I was totally out of my depth, yet I didn't know where to turn. I kept getting an image in my mind of a stained-glass window in an old Gothic cathedral. This was my only association with the term *exorcism* at the time. With nothing else to go on, I decided to search among the dusty shelves of antique bookstores for anything I could find on medieval exorcisms.

It was in one of these bookstores that I happened upon an illustration of Archangel Michael in a brilliant stained-glass panel of an English church. The gilt-edged book mentioned prayers for calling upon the archangel's assistance when dealing with "daemons." I noticed I'd been holding my breath for a long time and was starting to sweat. This was the nearest I'd come to a description of how to exorcise a haunted house.

The book said: "Michael is the prince of the heavenly armies. The faithful call upon him in all dangers of soul and body and implore his intercession at the hour of death that their souls may by him be brought before the throne of God."

As I jotted down these words, I could no longer deny the reality and extent of the haunting, and I understood how truly helpless we were. I'd been thinking that I somehow had the power to make a stand to protect my family amid the swirling legions that moved at liberty through our house each night. I was in way over my head, but Michael was throwing me a lifeline. I began to breathe through my tears.

I'd been raised in a diluted Christian tradition, which placed no emphasis on the dramatic presence of archangels. Now as I stood in that old bookshop that morning, gazing at the image of Michael aiming his mighty spear at the terrible beast pinned under his shoe, I knew that I'd found the right man for the job.

That night, my son was away at a sleepover. I got into bed and closed my eyes. It was time. The room was icy cold, and the whole house was twitchy and tense, as always. Not sure what to do next, I simply said a prayer to Archangel Michael, appealing for help. He instantly appeared in my mind's eye as a tall, fiery figure. I actually felt his warmth fill the room and was immediately comforted by his presence.

I asked him to please help me get rid of the ghosts or entities that were in our house. As soon as I mentioned them, I saw—like a movie screen in my mind's eye—a great number of shapes gathering in the darkness before me.

Archangel Michael stood in front of me, shielding me with his great wings and huge aura of burning white light. The souls that had gathered before him seemed calm in his presence. I then noticed that he was directing them to move off to the right, where a small opening of light was growing brighter.

It was as if a heavy stone was being rolled away from an entrance to the side of a mountain, and we were all watching from inside the cave as the glowing rays of the sun streamed in to warm us. The golden white light shining through that opening seemed to beckon to the huddled spirits inside. All I could do was watch as Archangel Michael directed them one by one to walk through that door into the brilliant sunshine.

As the line of shadowy souls moved toward and through the lighted doorway, more and more kept coming! This procession seemed to go on and on for a very long time, and although I felt myself drifting off to sleep, I fought to stay awake to see what would happen next.

The archangel must have sensed my fatigue. He commanded those who had not yet passed through the lighted door to go away for now and leave me in peace. And at his direction, they simply melted away. It seemed that Archangel Michael had opened up a portal for all those lost souls to move through so that they would no longer be restless and stuck in a place where they didn't belong. And all this was done without any battle, in the most peaceful, compassionate way.

The energy in our house quickly settled down, and the archangel returned many times to usher these souls away into the light. Whenever he appeared, they seemed to come from miles around to stand in an orderly line and move into the light he'd provided for them. In time, Michael no longer needed to visit so regularly, and our house began to feel more like a home.

I was later told by a local that the land near the top of that hill had probably once been an ancient burial ground. And the house itself stood just a few blocks away from an existing cemetery dating back to the earliest settlers. Evidently, Archangel Michael had called out to a vast number of souls, including those who died centuries ago, to move into the light.

We had some very happy years in that house. Much later, after reviving the beautiful gardens and renovating the property with great care, I sold that house on the hill for a record price. And by this time, thanks to Michael's work, small children could be heard playing happily in the neighborhood. Thank you, Archangel Michael!

As we've seen, Archangel Michael's specialty involves protecting us and releasing fear and its causes. He does whatever it takes to help us feel safe and peaceful, and sometimes that means he ventures into the area of physical healing, working in tandem with the Archangel of Healing, Raphael, as we'll explore in the next chapter.

CHAPTER EIGHT

ARCHANGELS MICHAEL
AND RAPHAEL

Archangel Michael's methods for healing, as discussed in Chapter 7, are powerful and effective. In fact, many people report immediate relief from pain and fear when they ask for his help. While we don't normally think of Michael as a "healing" angel, his work definitely has that result, as this story from Sandee Belen illustrates:

> When I was younger, I used to be a dancer but always had problems with my right foot. Occasionally, the muscles would tighten up and lock, causing extreme pain. One night when I experienced a sharp pain in my foot, I got sick of it and called upon Archangel Michael to release whatever metaphysical cause I was holding on to that created the effect of discomfort in this area. It immediately ceased!

I've seen people instantly heal from chronic pain following Michael's intervention. That's because a lot of spinal and muscular pain stems from fear-based cords and negative energy. Once Michael removes these sources, it goes away.

However, most of the time when people want a physical healing, they call upon beings associated specifically with health such as Jesus, certain saints or deities, or Archangel Raphael.

Raphael's name means "he who heals" or "God heals." He appears in the Catholic canonical text the Book of Tobias as the angel who heals Tobias of blindness. Raphael also accompanies Tobias (or Tobit, as he's sometimes referred to) on his walking journey, which gives the angel the secondary specialty of being a helper of travelers.

Healing with the Archangels

Archangels Michael and Raphael work so well in tandem that their relationship feels akin to a best friendship. They truly complement each other's gifts, and together offer an unstoppable combination of powerful healing abilities.

I frequently receive miraculous healing stories about Michael and Raphael, such as this beautiful example from Beverly M. Czikowsky:

> My 14-year-old nephew was diagnosed with an aortic aneurysm as well as a blood-clotting disorder, so surgery was especially difficult and dangerous for him. As he went into it, we prayed

together. My brave nephew even entered the operating room singing!

The long procedure was a success, but the next day his condition worsened. As his body began to fill with fluid, his vitals declined and his breathing grew shallow. The doctor said he'd done all he could do and the only thing left was prayer. In my opinion, prayer is never a last resort—it is our maintenance.

We held hands as a family and formed a circle around my nephew's hospital bed. Together, we invoked the archangels Michael and Raphael, but we could feel the presence of many loving angels. We had a very specific request: "Please release this fluid from his body, heal him, and replace the fluid with your wondrous white light." The room was filled with love—it was real, tangible. Everyone's eyes were tear filled, including those of the ICU nurses.

The next morning the doctors were completely speechless. Overnight, my nephew had lost ten pounds of body fluid. The doctors couldn't provide a medical explanation. They said it was miraculous.

Was it miraculous? Perhaps, but *I* believe it was love, pure and simple. God and his angels are omnipresent.

Today, my nephew is a healthy guitar-playing, song-writing, outdoorsy 16-year-old . . . and I'm a very proud auntie!

No matter what the medical condition, calling upon Raphael and Michael can bring a calming presence to the patient, hospital room, and other aspects involved with healing. This next story from a friend of mine named Ariel Wolfe shows that Michael and Raphael's presence is even measurable on sensitive medical equipment:

> Recently I had to have a series of MRIs done for a health condition. I always ask that Michael and Raphael accompany me, so as I lay completely still in the MRI tube, I enjoyed the energy of these two angels as I told them how I was ready to be healthy.
>
> Then I saw Michael and Raphael begin to dance around me: The archangels were doing a circle dance over my midriff area while I was lying motionless on the narrow table in the narrow tube.
>
> Suddenly, the nurse's voice came through a speaker inside the MRI tube and announced, "We're detecting some motion in there! Remember, you have to lie quietly."
>
> "I swear I never moved a muscle!" I said, so happy to know that the angels' movement had been detected on the MRI.

I love Ariel's story because of the humor displayed by the angels and their ingenious way of letting her know that they were with her.

Although Raphael is the chief healing angel, it's always helpful to ask Michael to be involved in the face of any frightening situation. After all, he's wonderful at dissipating fear, and that's *always* healthy! That's why the following miraculous story from Susan Chorney is a beautiful example of how both archangels work together:

On August 14, 2004, my three stepchildren were involved in a car accident with their mother. My 13-year-old stepdaughter, Nicole, was in a coma with severe head injuries, a broken jaw, and a collapsed lung.

On the way to the airport to fly to the children's hospital, I knew that I needed help to get me through this tragic ordeal, so I grabbed Doreen's book *Archangels & Ascended Masters* so that my husband, Paul, and I could cling to some shred of hope that Nicole would live.

The doctors told us that she would probably not make it through the night. Over and over I surrounded her with white light, inviting archangels Raphael and Michael to heal her brain and lung and thanking them repeatedly for joining her.

Nicole had a probe in her brain that measured the swelling, and the higher the number, the more likely it was that she wouldn't survive. As God is my witness, when I would pray over her and invite Raphael and Michael to heal her, the swelling would come down. It was a scientific fact that was proven by the numbers on the monitor. This ray of hope kept my husband from despair. He never wanted me to leave her side!

Nicole has survived and is now in high school. The doctors say her recovery was unbelievable.

Paul acknowledges and appreciates everything Raphael and Michael did to such a degree that every day he talks to his angels. He now knows that whenever he needs help, it's just a matter of asking them.

Raphael guides healers in aiding their patients. He also helps students of the healing arts know which health-care specialty to choose, as well as offering guidance and support for education. In this next story, it's clear how Raphael and Michael provide assistance to healers during unnerving situations. After all, being a healer is a lot of responsibility and at times involves a great deal of pressure, as a registered nurse named Susan shares:

Little did I know that on my way back home to New York City from Angel Therapy Practitioner training, I'd have the opportunity to use my skills in a much-needed, almost life-and-death situation.

After 17 years of working as a registered nurse in the corporate world, evaluating medical records for clinical trials and adverse-event reports, I kept having the nagging desire to work directly with people again face-to-face.

During my flight, a message rang out over the loudspeaker requesting a doctor or nurse to identify themselves. After I identified myself as a nurse, a flight attendant asked me to follow her to the back galley to evaluate a woman who felt ill. As we walked quickly down the aisle, I secretly hoped that there was a doctor on board.

The other passengers scanned our faces to get a read on what was happening. I had to hold back the tears that came to my eyes as I entered the galley, and I wondered if I could help this lady in distress after my long absence from bedside nursing. I composed myself and found her sitting in the back with an oxygen mask on. With no tools, I had to rely on pure instinct—and help from God and the angels.

This lovely lady in her late 50s was seated, with her husband standing calmly nearby. Joan (not her real name) looked pale but was able to tell me briefly what was wrong. I checked her pulse but could only feel it faintly, so I tried the other wrist, only to find the same thing. I wondered what I could possibly do for her, especially when she began shaking with chills. She seemed to be getting worse. With no doctor in sight, it was clear that this one was for me and the angels.

I immediately invoked the emergency help of Heaven. I prayed hard and repeatedly for assistance from archangels Michael and Raphael to help me out and keep this lovely lady conscious until we landed. "Please don't let her faint!" I implored them.

I hoped that an emergency landing wouldn't be necessary, especially since Joan's legs had buckled earlier as she'd made her way to the back of the plane. And with nearly four hours of the flight left and no other assistance on board, I relied heavily on angelic support. As her chills worsened and the blankets weren't enough, I couldn't think of how to warm this lady up.

Praying intensely for help, I felt the Divinely guided inspiration to reach across the galley and grab a few of the heated breakfast sandwiches (just ready to be distributed to the passengers) and place them across Joan's shoulders and in her hands. It worked! She drank down some warm tea, and slowly the color came back to her face and the shaking stopped. *Thank you, angels!* I said inside my mind.

I then spoke to the airplane captain, who called a medical doctor at my request as things were settling down. In the end, the lady made it through the flight and walked off the plane without assistance or fanfare. There were a few paramedics and airport police just outside on the runway to check that all was well.

When I got off the plane, I strongly felt that God had put me back to work face-to-face with people. After all, I'd prayed for it! And with angelic support, it was a very successful intervention. Thank goodness for Michael and Raphael. I really couldn't have done it without them.

Reading Susan's story, you can imagine how much pressure she was under as the sole health-care practitioner on the airplane. Fortunately, Michael provides confidence and courage while Raphael gives specific healing guidance. They're certainly a winning combination to work with during any challenging situation.

Raphael and Michael to the Rescue!

The archangels have helped people in many situations, in addition to their collaborative healing work. As Chapter 6 described, Michael is brilliant at fixing mechanical and electrical items. Well, in this next story from Deanne Millett, he got a little help from Raphael during a repair intervention:

> Our car was constantly in the shop with problems, until finally the mechanic said that we'd need to replace the transmission. We couldn't afford this expense, so I prayed and asked Michael and Raphael to fix our car.
>
> In my mind's eye, I could see both angels bent over the car's engine, pulling things out and replacing them. They both had their sleeves rolled up and their wings tucked back. The next day the mechanic told me that the transmission was fine and only minor repairs to the car were necessary. Thank you, Michael and Raphael!

Raphael's primary role is to mend physical bodies and support professional healers; however, in this case, Deanne's financial fears were healed by his intervention. Both archangels are compassionate healers of emotions, because Raphael realizes that stress reduction is the best preventive medicine, as a college student named Julie Schwaiger discovered:

> I work two jobs and am in college part-time. My schedule is very exhausting, but I have to

keep this pace up for a few more years, so I take good care of myself.

Yet, once when I was particularly tired and on the verge of becoming sick, I was walking from my car to class and simply couldn't make it. I was ready to give up. I was so exhausted; plus, that particular teacher was somewhat difficult to get along with, and I felt emotionally vulnerable.

So, I asked archangels Michael and Raphael to help me make it to class and protect me from the professor. Right when I did so, I actually felt two presences walking with me and lifting me up so that my feet barely touched the ground. I also felt arms around my shoulders from either side of me, as if they were comforting me as well as holding me up.

I was inspired enough by this experience to muster my courage and go to class. And you know what? The teacher left me alone! She didn't even pick on anyone that day! Since that moment, I pray for protection every day!

The archangels are responsive to our calls for help, and that includes when we ask them to assist with another person, as we'll explore in the next chapter.

CALLING ON MICHAEL ON BEHALF OF SOMEONE ELSE

Michael can't violate a person's free will. Therefore, you have to ask for his assistance before he's allowed to intervene. The only exception is if people are in mortal danger before it's their time, and even then most have to follow Michael's guidance (using their own freewill decisions) in order to experience an intervention.

So the question invariably arises: *Is it okay to ask Archangel Michael to help others, or is that a violation of their free will?*

The answer is twofold:

1. When you call angels to another person's side, their *presence* is healing and calming, even if they don't directly intervene into the individual's life.

2. The angels are allowed to intervene in any situation to the degree to which it affects *you.*

As an example of the second point, let's say that you're worried about, and physically affected by, your spouse's cigarette smoking. When you ask the angels to help with this situation, they're allowed to do so with the aspects directly involving you, such as keeping the smoke away and boosting your inner peace and faith. While they can't force your partner to quit smoking, their presence may calm him or her enough that the desire for cigarettes is reduced or eliminated.

It's a good idea to ask Archangel Michael to watch over your loved ones, as this story from Debbie Allen illustrates:

> For almost a year, my husband has owned and driven a ten-ton truck for a living. Every morning as he leaves, I ask Archangel Michael to surround him in light and keep him safe, protected, and Divinely guided throughout the day. I also ask that his truck be surrounded by Divine light and angels, keeping the load safe. I then request that the angels remind other drivers to give the truck plenty of room on the road.
>
> I know that Archangel Michael has protected my husband, and three incidents really stand out to prove this.
>
> There was the time when he was entering a road and out of the corner of his eye, he saw a car racing toward him. My husband slammed on his brakes and braced himself for the inevitable collision. He watched as the three teenage passengers and driver slid toward his truck. To the shock of everyone involved, the car skidded

to a halt a mere hair's breadth away from the side of the truck!

On another occasion, my husband was rear-ended by a car, but no one was hurt and there was no damage to either vehicle!

The latest incident happened the day before a new insurance policy was due to take effect on the truck. We had received a rate half the price we'd been paying with our current insurance company, but it was conditional, based on the fact that we had never made a claim.

My husband called me with the news that a woman was claiming he'd hit the side of her car. He was unaware of having hit anyone, and upon reporting the incident at the police station, he was told that a police officer had witnessed the accident and believed he was at fault. It seemed clear-cut that he'd be held responsible, and our insurance premiums would almost double in cost.

I remembered the previous incident, though, and decided not to lose faith. I didn't know how, but I was sure Archangel Michael wouldn't let me down. That night, I arrived home just as my husband was hanging up the phone. "You'll never guess what's happened!" he exclaimed. Apparently, the woman had said that since there was no damage to her vehicle, she wanted to forget about the whole thing.

Since Michael is so adept at repairing automobiles, it's not surprising that his prayers for this type of intervention are instantly answered, even if it's on behalf of another person, as Rebecca Guthrie experienced:

> My friend called me and was quite distressed. She'd stopped at a rest area, and when she tried to leave, her car wouldn't start. It was getting late, and she was upset about being stuck there until midnight waiting for the roadside mechanic to turn up.
>
> My friend knew that I had a strong connection to the angels, so she contacted me to request that they help her. I asked if she'd called upon Archangel Michael to start her car. Yes, she said, but it hadn't worked.
>
> I immediately called upon Michael to fix the car and saw him bending over the engine, working on it. When I saw that he was finished, I asked her to start it; however, it still wouldn't turn over. I knew that she doubted the angels' ability to repair the car, and her lack of faith was preventing it from starting.
>
> I asked her to be willing to release her doubt and to trust in the angels. She was quiet for about a minute as she surrendered the entire situation to God. When she told me she was ready, I asked her to start the car. This time, it worked right away! She was absolutely blown away, and it was a beautiful reminder for me that with faith all things are possible.
>
> Michael has also assisted my partner and me many times with mechanical and computer issues. He's helped me connect my home entertainment

system and also set up broadband by showing me step-by-step instructions through pictures in my head.

As Rebecca's story illustrates, Michael's helpfulness boosted her friend's faith, which is what I believe is a major motivation behind the archangel's repair work. Notice how Rebecca did her part by following his guidance, which came to her as mental pictures. Other people may receive this input as intuitive feelings or through insights or ideas.

This next story from a woman named Li Ann shows how Michael's assistance defies normal logic:

> I was new to working with angels and was focusing on Archangel Michael because I was familiar with his name and thought that he oversaw all of the other angels.
>
> A friend who knew about my angelic connection called to ask me to pray on her behalf because she'd lost her car key the evening before. She was being driven to her vehicle to try to program the correct code into a blank replacement key. I prayed: "I give thanks that Archangel Michael and any other angels are with my friends to ensure that they have a safe trip and that the car starts instantly."
>
> My friend said that her blank car key had never been programmed before, so she was reading the instructions on the drive to the car. A little bit later she called me to inquire whether I'd called upon Archangel Michael. When I said

yes, she asked me to explain the exact nature of my prayer. I did, and then asked my friend why she wanted to know.

She replied, "You're not going to believe what happened here. I've been studying the coding instructions the whole ride down here for an hour. When we drove up to the car, I opened the unlocked door, put the key in the ignition—and this is a blank, uncoded key—and the car instantly started without my having to do a thing!"

Elated to hear the story, I said, "Well, the angels took care of it! Wow!" Since this was my first angel experience (to my knowledge), I was so glad to get the validation from my friend, and I'm sure to continue working with Michael and the other angels after this!

Archangel Michael has many talents, as we've seen so far, including protection, repairs, and healing. While the other archangels each have specialties, we could safely and with great respect say that Michael is an "all-purpose angel" to call upon during any circumstance.

We usually think of St. Anthony or Archangel Chamuel when it comes to finding lost objects, but as this chapter's stories illustrate, Michael is also well versed in locating items.

If *you* are looking for a missing object, the following story may serve as an example of what happens when you ask for Archangel Michael's help. Susan Gunton discovered that Michael could find lost items even when she called on him on behalf of another person:

I work with a man who was quite skeptical about angels. One day he was busily searching for some receipts so that he could be reimbursed. He was desperate to find them because he'd spent a lot of his personal money for company expenses.

I told him a few times to ask the angels for help. I said, "If you don't know which to call upon for a specific purpose, you can always ask Archangel Michael because he helps with *everything.*" Well, to my surprise, he later called me to say that he had indeed asked Michael to help him find the receipts. He'd gone home and immediately found them in a place where he never would have looked. He was quite excited!

When he returned to the office, he even told our supervisor what had transpired and how he had found his receipts. He now asks Archangel Michael for help all the time!

My mother also works with Archangel Michael to find lost objects. For example, she had been looking for her gloves for a couple of weeks. I suggested that she ask Michael to help her find them. As soon as she did, she got an idea to get a reserve can of coffee from a cupboard, a place where she would never have had reason to think her gloves would be. Lo and behold, there they were in the cupboard right beside the coffee! She now asks for help a lot more.

Calling upon Archangel Michael on behalf of someone else is a loving gesture on your part, with no potential negative side effects! And who knows? Another person may return the favor for you one day, as Anne Davey discovered:

> I'd recently given a dear friend an oracle card with a painting of Archangel Michael on it as a reminder that this powerful angel takes wonderful care of us.
>
> Around the same time, I began struggling with money. My healing practice just wasn't making me enough income. I was sad to go back to a regular job, as I loved what I was doing. When I was leaving for work one day, this same dear friend told me that she'd asked Archangel Michael to help me with my work situation. Within the week, a totally new position called a "wellness coordinator" was created in my workplace. The job description seemed tailor-made for me. I applied and was appointed to the role! Thank you, Archangel Michael.

Anne found her perfect job with the help of Archangel Michael, and in the next chapter, we'll look at the other things he helps us find, too.

CHAPTER TEN

MICHAEL'S HELP WITH CAREER AND LIFE PURPOSE

Those who are on the spiritual path and work with angels tend to be sensitive individuals who prefer the companionship of gentle people and devote time to meaningful and pleasant activities. So it's no wonder that many spiritually minded individuals desire a pleasurable career with these same qualities of gentleness and meaningfulness. Most want to contribute something of value to the world, such as providing help and healing for people, the environment, animals, or some other cause.

Archangel Michael is the go-to angel for any aspect of your career and life purpose. He has access to your Akashic records (or "Book of Life"), which reveal the soul plan that you have for this lifetime. If you've forgotten what your purpose is or you're insecure about whether or not you're on the right path, Michael can help.

I recommend going to a quiet place with a pad of paper and a pen and having a question-and-answer session with

Michael. First, ask him to write his messages through your pen and to ensure that only his Divine voice comes through. Then jot down a query about your career and record whatever impressions—such as thoughts, ideas, visions, or words—come to you.

If you're unsure whether these impressions are your imagination, write a question to the archangel: "How do I know this is really you talking to me?" You'll know from his reply that his messages are quite real.

You can also ask Michael to give you signs to guide you on the right professional path and to help you with financial security during career changes.

Michael is especially helpful for those who are leaving a secure but disliked job in order to pursue self-employment or a dream career, as Claire Jennings discovered:

> It's always been my dream to run a meta-physical store, yet as a single mother with two small children, I needed a steady income. So I asked Archangel Michael for guidance, and I got the strong message to begin with an eBay store and then move on to selling at weekend outdoor-market stalls.
>
> Well, I could easily accept the eBay guidance, but the outdoor-market advice just didn't make sense to me. I kept thinking, *First I need to build up my inventory of products; then I'll be ready to have a stall!* Obviously, Michael was right, and my doubts were coming from my ego!
>
> I kept resisting the ongoing intuitive guidance to have a market stall, always arguing with Michael

that I didn't have enough products to sell. Finally, I heard his voice as clear as day: "Spread it out!" It took me a minute to understand that he meant to spread my products out on a table. When I did, I realized that I had more than enough stock for a stall.

That night, I had a dream visit from Archangel Michael, who was pouring a giant cornucopia of coins on my head. I began selling at the market . . . and it's very fun, fulfilling, and prosperous. And since I started my stall, my eBay sales have dramatically increased as well!

I feel as if I'm propelled by Michael and he's gently nudging me along. Every time I'm hesitant about an idea that "pops" into my head, my sales slow. When I listen to these Divinely inspired ideas, I get a surge in sales, like a reward.

Claire's story illustrates how the archangel gives reliable career guidance that yields emotional and financial rewards. It's normal to resist or feel intimidated when he encourages you to move in the direction of your dreams. The human ego says, "I'm not qualified!" or "I don't deserve happiness" when doors of opportunity open. Fortunately, Archangel Michael walks through them with you, lending you support and confidence, as a woman named Maree experienced:

I worked in a laboratory for nearly six years processing soil samples for a worldwide mining company. Since my job wasn't exactly Earth friendly, I became increasingly unhappy and frustrated with it. It just wasn't *me* anymore!

One day I was so overcome with fatigue and stress that I cried out in my mind: *Angels, help me! I want out of this job!* I had never begged for anything so much in my life!

Weeks went by and I continually asked, "Michael, please let me know when it's time for me to leave this job. Tell me when I can financially afford to do so."

On the day my prayer was answered, the most powerful, peaceful, and calm feeling overcame me. These sensations originated from my heart, and I suddenly saw Michael before my very eyes! All he said is: "It's time." I didn't know whether to laugh or cry!

Two days later I handed in my resignation; and that peaceful, calm feeling didn't leave me for several days. I just knew deep down that this was definitely the right thing for me to do, and there was absolutely no doubt in my heart and mind that the guidance came from Archangel Michael.

That was 13 months ago, and not only have I found myself again, but I've also opened up my spiritual abilities. And if that isn't enough, I've finally worked out what my life purpose is! All I can say is that Archangel Michael is a girl's best friend—much better than any diamond! Quite simply, he's my best mate.

Michael's guidance extends to day-to-day career activities, too. A woman named Helen learned firsthand that he could ensure good timing when making business phone calls:

My manager and I work in a very small office in Canada. Most of what we do involves contacting isolated northern communities. Because of the harsh weather conditions, telephone lines and the equipment servicing these communities often fail, making it a challenge for us to meet our deadlines.

Recently, though, I've begun invoking Archangel Michael to make sure that the communities receive their information. It works so well that my manager noticed that something must have changed, as we seemed to be having fewer communication problems than before. I told her about asking for Archangel Michael's help, and she seemed open to it and said that she thought it was a great idea!

A week later we had an emergency deadline, and paperwork needed to be signed by certain members of 50 communities within three days. So I asked for Archangel Michael's help, and things were moving along smoothly and at an incredible pace!

On the last day before the deadline, we had one community left. My manager tried to contact the person who needed to sign the contract, but there was no response. She had multiple phone numbers for this person, so she left messages where she could but still was unable to reach him.

Then she thought of Archangel Michael, asked for his help, and started dialing. This time, she was able to connect with the person, the papers were signed prior to the deadline, and everything worked out perfectly.

We frequently spend more time with our co-workers than with our family and friends, so it's reassuring to know that Michael helps heal and harmonize our professional relationships, as a woman named Lisa Toplis discovered:

I'd just started working part-time in an office I shared with a guy who made me feel very uncomfortable. I'd taken over the part of his job that he was too busy to squeeze in among his other duties. As soon as I started in the role, though, I could sense anger and resentment from him. Every time I tried to fulfill a task, he'd make patronizing and condescending statements.

I didn't want to harbor bad feelings toward this guy, but it was very difficult to ignore him. We worked together in such a confined area that I couldn't see how to escape the situation. When at the beginning of the third week I realized that the problem was going to continue, I silently asked Archangel Michael to help me. I mentally said: *Dear Michael, I'd really appreciate your help on this issue, as I'm stuck in close proximity to this guy and can't ignore him. I don't wish to feel this way about my job, him, or myself.*

The next week when I returned to the office, a true miracle occurred: I was given my own office! The daily office manager appeared by my desk and said, "Lisa, you look really cramped in that space—let me rethink this." A few hours later, I was installed in the sales director's office, in comfort and isolation. (The sales director was out with prospects and only came to the office on rare occasions.) I could make phone calls and function in peace!

I'm so grateful to Archangel Michael for rescuing me from an awkward and unpleasant situation—and doing it so quickly, with exactly the right result. As a part-timer, I would never have dreamed of getting my own office in a very cramped work environment. When Archangel Michael helps, though, things certainly turn out far better than you could have imagined!

If you're dreaming of leaving your current job to pursue something more fulfilling, then you'll feel inspired by the next two stories, which involve people who were helped to do just that. As you read Annelies Hoornik's experience, keep in mind that Archangel Michael can provide similar career assistance for you:

I was feeling a lot of stress in my computer-software job, since my company had laid off many of their employees and I was doing the work of nine people. I'd heard that meditation helped with stress management, so I decided to give it a try.

After three weeks of daily meditations, I had a profound experience! I felt myself lift off of my couch and move into surroundings that were filled with bright white light. I saw three steps leading up to a patio. A friendly looking man stood in it, and he began walking toward me. I could see that his clothing was very casual, but his face was obscured by the bright light.

He said that he wanted to show me something, and he held out his hand to me. I took it, as he seemed trustworthy and nice. But when he turned to walk ahead of me, I saw huge white wings protruding from his back. This frightened me because I'd learned as a child that angels take you away when you die. So I willed myself to be alive and back on my living-room couch, and that's exactly what instantly happened.

I *knew* that I had met Archangel Michael. No one told me—I just knew. I also knew that he wasn't taking me to die and that it was safe for me to contact him again. So the next day, I sat down to meditate and decided to see if Michael would come again. I didn't know what to expect, since I had no experience with angels. I just sat down, meditated, and sent out the message that if he was still out there and willing to show me what he'd come for the previous day, *I* was willing to go and see it.

It took about a split second and I was back with Michael in those white surroundings again. He showed me a special place to meditate and find peace of mind. In the following days and weeks, I spent a lot of time in the white place and saw a great deal. Michael introduced me to my guardian angel, two healing angels, and the other archangels.

Archangel Michael was very clear that I needed to stop working in the software industry and start a full-time healing practice. He said that I would do so before May 1, 2002. Every vision that the archangel showed me has come true, including my healing practice, which opened on April 29, 2002. My life is so much happier because of the constant guidance of Archangel Michael. It's so satisfying to help people heal, and I can't imagine doing anything else.

By assisting with Annelies's career, Archangel Michael actually helped all of the people who benefit from her healing practice. Notice the happiness Annelies expresses, since this is one of the chief reasons why Michael aids us on our career path. Her joy is also an indicator that she is on the right one, since our Divine life purpose is always meaningful and pleasurable.

Michael has taught me that everyone has unique talents and gifts that can be used in service of the world. When you're working in a field that matches your interests, your work is joyful *and* successful. The old belief that you must suffer to earn money is puritanical and outmoded. We're entering a new phase of our collective spiritual path in which everyone will be employed in careers connected to their natural talents, passions, and interests. And Archangel Michael is overseeing this positive and healthy shift.

An angel therapist named Valerie Camozzi is living proof that when it comes to career guidance, Archangel Michael is hands down the best life coach around:

I worked as a registered nurse for 25 years in newborn and pediatric intensive care. I love working with infants and their families, and attending a birth was the highlight of my job. As much as I enjoyed my work, though, my nursing career was becoming less satisfying. I felt a void.

My heart lay in teaching others to use their intuitive abilities to connect with and hear their angels. I was feeling less and less connected to my work at the hospital. Before I fell asleep one night, I asked Archangel Michael for help. I told him that I loved working with families and babies but that I wasn't happy at work anymore.

The next morning, I felt as though I'd slept for a week. I didn't remember any dreams. As I got up, I experienced a deep sense of peace, had energy, and was happy. I went for a hike, and when I returned, I heard a voice in my head that told me to go to the computer. I sat down at it and typed my letter of resignation to the hospital. I dated it, signed it, and put it in the mail. To this day I don't remember what I wrote. My nurse manager said that the letter touched her deeply and that although she was sad to see me leave, she understood and wished me well.

I believe that Archangel Michael dictated my letter of resignation at the computer that day. I feel that he gave me the courage to leave a job I'd done for so many years. I now teach classes about angels, intuitive development, meditation, and energy healing full-time. I continue to attend deliveries privately as a birth coach for parents, too.

Afterword

God intends for us to have peaceful, meaningful, and happy lives—just as all parents want for their offspring. The angels are our Creator's gift to each of us to guide and protect us along the way. Just as we want the gifts that we give to be enjoyed by their recipient, so too does the Divine aim for us to enjoy the gift of the angels.

If you agree with the premise that God is 100 percent love, then it's impossible for the Creator to know anything *but* love. Yet, human existence often seems to have a lower percentage of this feeling in daily life. The angels are the bridge between God's truth of complete love and the human experience of drama and pain. The angels can see both the spiritual truth and the ego-illusions, so into the human dream they bring Heaven's pure light, love, and wisdom.

As the overseer of the angels, Michael is Earth's representative of the all-encompassing strength of the Divine. He demonstrates that with spiritual faith, all things are possible. He helps us all live in God's world of purity and divinity upon the earth.

Michael is the embodiment of compassion, as he assists everyone with whatever is needed. He never judges a person's "worthiness." He simply says yes to whatever instills safety and peace.

Michael is wisdom in action. His miraculous solutions, guidance, interventions, and healings are completely ingenious. For each crisis, he has the perfect solution, created in a split second of time. This is one reason why you needn't worry about *how* the archangel will help you or hand him a script to follow. Just ask for his help and then leave the solution to him.

Michael is a steady reminder of God's presence on Earth. At times, you may feel alone or abandoned, yet all you have to do is think the archangel's name and he's there. Breathe and feel the warmth of his presence, and notice the ideas and visions that come to you from his guidance.

Michael lends you support, courage, and confidence. If you are, or are considering, making a life change, then be sure to ask him to be with you all along the way. He'll boost your resolve to make healthy changes, as well as guide you to new opportunities and help you heal from past experiences.

You can ask Archangel Michael to live with you, if you'd like. Since he's completely unfettered, unlimited, and omnipresent, he can be with every person who asks for his presence.

You can also invite him into your dreams, as your nighttime mind is much calmer and more open to angels than your busy daytime one. As you're falling asleep, ask Michael for whatever guidance or healing you'd like. When you wake up, you may not remember what transpired during the night, but you'll know that you've shifted for the better.

Whether you prefer to ask God to send Michael to your side or you talk directly to the archangel instead, know that asking for his help is a step toward creating peace on Earth, one person at a time . . . beginning with *you.*

Remember that God and Archangel Michael love you unconditionally. They see your Divine magnificence, your talents, your goodness, and your radiant light. To them you are an Earth angel, and they're very happy to support you as you fulfill your angelic mission. Enjoy the process! Your joy lifts your own heart as well as those around you!

With love,
Doreen

ABOUT THE AUTHOR

Doreen Virtue holds B.A., M.A., and Ph.D. degrees in counseling psychology; and is a lifelong clairvoyant who works with the angelic realm. She is the author of the *Healing with the Angels* book and oracle cards; *Archangels & Ascended Masters;* and *Angel Therapy®,* among other works. Her products are available in most languages worldwide.

Doreen has appeared on *Oprah,* CNN, *The View,* and other television and radio programs. She writes regular columns for *Woman's World, New Age Retailer,* and *Spirit & Destiny* magazines. For more information on Doreen and the workshops she presents, please visit **www.AngelTherapy.com.**

You can listen to Doreen's live weekly radio show, and call her for a reading, by visiting **HayHouseRadio.com®.**

NOTES

NOTES

NOTES

NOTES

NOTES

NOTES

NOTES

NOTES

HAY HOUSE TITLES OF RELATED INTEREST

❧ ❧ ❧

We hope you enjoyed this Hay House book. If you'd like to receive our online catalog featuring additional information on Hay House books and products, or if you'd like to find out more about the Hay Foundation, please contact:

Hay House, Inc.
P.O. Box 5100
Carlsbad, CA 92018-5100

(760) 431-7695 or **(800) 654-5126**
(760) 431-6948 (fax) or **(800) 650-5115 (fax)**
www.hayhouse.com® • **www.hayfoundation.org**

❧ ❧ ❧

Published and distributed in Australia by: Hay House Australia Pty. Ltd., 18/36 Ralph St., Alexandria NSW 2015 • *Phone:* 612-9669-4299 *Fax:* 612-9669-4144 • www.hayhouse.com.au

Published and distributed in the United Kingdom by: Hay House UK, Ltd., 292B Kensal Rd., London W10 5BE • *Phone:* 44-20-8962-1230 *Fax:* 44-20-8962-1239 • www.hayhouse.co.uk

Published and distributed in the Republic of South Africa by: Hay House SA (Pty), Ltd., P.O. Box 990, Witkoppen 2068 • *Phone/Fax:* 27-11-467-8904 • info@hayhouse.co.za • www.hayhouse.co.za

Published in India by: Hay House Publishers India, Muskaan Complex, Plot No. 3, B-2, Vasant Kunj, New Delhi 110 070 *Phone:* 91-11-4176-1620 • *Fax:* 91-11-4176-1630 • www.hayhouse.co.in

Distributed in Canada by: Raincoast, 9050 Shaughnessy St., Vancouver, B.C. V6P 6E5 *Phone:* (604) 323-7100 • *Fax:* (604) 323-2600 • www.raincoast.com

❧ ❧ ❧

Take Your Soul on a Vacation

Visit **www.HealYourLife.com**® to regroup, recharge, and reconnect with your own magnificence. Featuring blogs, mind-body-spirit news, and life-changing wisdom from Louise Hay and friends.

Visit **www.HealYourLife.com** today!